How to Be a Couple & Still Be Free

TINA B. TESSINA, MA

RILEY K. SMITH, MA

NEWCASTLE PUBLISHNG CO., INC.

NORTH HOLLYWOOD, CALIFORNIA

1987

Edited by Douglas Menville.

This is an expanded, updated edition of the book originally published
in 1980, with a new chapter added.

A NEWCASTLE ORIGINAL
First Printing October 1980
8 9 10
Printed in the United States of America

Tina dedicates this book to:
Denton Roberts, who planted the seed
Jerry Wildau, who helped pull the weeds,
Richard Sharrard,
    who is helping to reap the harvest.

Riley dedicates this book to:
Our students, teachers, and friends,
most of whom are all three.

I know you—

I have seen you weep,
and been seen.
When the laughter rises
from your center place
I join you in song.

With you . . .

I have loved,
    angered,
      rested,
        feared.

We've explored . . .

    new worlds
    new selves
    new silences
    new distances
    —a new language of sharing.

In the creation of

    my newest life
    and my oldest history
       . . . you are.

A miracle:

> we fight.
> we throw small things
> and great sharp words
> . . . and we do not break.

You push, goad,

> love, support . . .
> I resist.

We pause, and look!
a new vista!

In the end, we create:

> meaning in struggle
> joy in success
> peace in security
> and love—
> > surpassing our shining selves.

You are all my wishes, all my speculations

> . . . granted.

I know you.
I am known.

In that certainty is freedom.

CONTENTS

TINA'S FOREWORD

Love is a confusing word. We use it to mean obligation: "If you love me you'll. . . ." We use it for dependency: "I love you, I can't live without you." We use it for owner-ship: "We're in love, we belong to each other." We use it for charity: "I do this for you because I love you."

I want to see love freed. I think the world exists on love, and that it is love which binds us together.

Science has not yet understood the mysterious force which holds the tiny particles of the atom together, and thus holds everything in our physical world together.

Pretend with me that the binding force is love, and see where that thought goes. If that were true—then we'd each be an expression of love and surrounded by love. The phrase "God is love" would take on new dimensions.

We would be free and able to let our partners be free, because we would not have to do anything to be bonded. And we would not have to prove to ourselves that we love—it would be obvious all around us. We could let our partners be different without being scared—just as protons and neutrons are different and express them-selves differently, yet remain bonded.

So this book is about freeing love. I think love grows out of freedom, that free beings are open to loving and being loved. It is not possible to push or force people into loving. The only thing that works is leaving enough room for love to grow.

Riley and I have found some ways to be free and we share them with you, because the more free people there are, the more love will be freed in the world.

Tina B. Tessina

RILEY'S FOREWORD

I believe that people who are exploring freedom in their couple relationships are actually exploring a new level of love—

> love that doesn't limit the beloved.
>
> love that is not possessive.
>
> love that encourages growth and satisfaction in the beloved.
>
> love that rejoices at the beloved's joy.

We're beginners.
What we are doing violates the traditional rules and we have no model to follow.

So, not only are we struggling to shed our indoctrination, but we are having to create unprecedented concepts and methods.

Let us support one another.
Let us teach one another.
Let us love one another—
without expectations.

Riley K. Smith

AUTHORS NOTE: We believe that men and women are potentially equal in all areas. We believe that the use of the masculine pronoun to designate men and women together (e.g., "each person, during *his* life . . .") is a subtle and pervasive denial of this equality. Therefore, whenever possible throughout this book, we will use the words "one," "they" or "their" as neutral gender pronouns instead of "his." Even though they may sound a bit clumsy and their usage not considered grammatically correct by strict standards, after all, this *is* a book about freedom. . . .

*This book
is about options.
Please feel free.*

THERE'S A BIAS IN THIS BOOK

And here it is. Up front.

1. The health, happiness and growth of any individual is more important than the health, happiness and growth of any couple or group (including family and nation). Not the other way around.

2. A healthy, happy and dynamic couple or group will enhance the growth of the individuals in it.

3. If a couple or a group isn't healthy, happy and dynamic, it should change in some positive way for the sake of the individuals in it.

4. The individuals in a couple or group can consciously make the couple or group what they want to be.
It takes loving, thoughtful effort.
And it's well worth it.

We encourage you, our reader, to allow us our bias as we allow you yours. You are welcome to take from our book what you want. The rest you can adapt to suit yourself or leave behind. . . .

SECTION I

FREEDOM
&
INTIMACY

.

CHAPTER 1

BEING FREE

This first chapter is a definition of freedom. It is biased. You are free to make your own list if ours doesn't suit you (actually we recommend that you do).

The point is to know what YOU mean when YOU say "freedom."

Being free is setting my own boundaries.

Being free is being *me*.

Being free is:
  sleeping when I'm sleepy.
  eating when I'm hungry.
  being separate when I want to be.
  being together when I want to be.
  touching when I want to touch.
  being touched when it feels good to me.
  being touched where it feels good to me.
  doing work I enjoy.
  taking the kind of vacation I like.
  exercising when I want to.
  following my curiosity.
  loving.

saying no as easily as saying yes.
acknowledging my anger.
acknowledging my sadness, fear and joy.
being funny.
being serious.
being excited.
being mellow.
being energetic.
being tired.
being vulnerable.
being needy.
being powerful.
being competent.
being responsible for my life.
being responsible to me.
flowing with the present.

BEING FREE IS *NOT* BEING SELFISH!

Being free is NOT:
    ignoring others.
    taking without giving.
    being irresponsible.
    being lonely.

Being free is NOT living in the past.
Being free is NOT living for the future.

Being free is not necessarily:
    being alone.
    "playing the field."
    moving from place to place.

Being free is living according to who I am now, instead of
who I ought to be, was, or will be.

So being free begins with three things:
discovering the rules for how I ought to be,

Being free
is
being me.

discovering who I am,
and separating them so that I know the difference.

For most of us who opt for freedom *and* intimacy this is an exciting, continuous process that takes a lot of time and energy. There are tough times and easy times, joyful times and painful times, alone times and profoundly together times.

It's not an easy journey, but the rewards are magnificent.

This book is a guide for this journey for people in couples.

CHAPTER 2

BEING A COUPLE

A couple is two people who are committed to being with each other more intensely and/or more often than with others.

This usually implies a degree of love and intimate contact.

It could be a dating relationship, living together, married or not.

It could be open or closed sexually.

There are a lot of reasons for coupling. Many of them are cultural and we'll discuss that in the next chapter.

One reason that seems universal is that the couple relationship is conducive to intimacy. So the chapter on Being a Couple becomes a chapter on intimacy.

Here are some of the things that intimacy is or can be:

Intimacy is being close.
Intimacy is no secrets.
Intimacy is:
>   melding together
>   merging our bodies.
>   merging our minds.

    merging our spirits.
    being sexy together.
    sharing our feelings.
    sharing our beliefs.
    me knowing you and
       you knowing me.

We need intimacy just as we need food and shelter. And just as with food and shelter, no one needs it all the time and some people need more than others.

It is possible to be a couple without intimacy.

It is also possible to have intimate contact without being a couple.

We believe, however, that intimate contact is the main reason (other than cultural) people couple up.

There are two things available in a couple relationship that make this so.

One, it takes less energy and decision-making to have intimacy in a couple relationship. For one thing, it doesn't take much planning to get together. For another, Mom and Dad and the world say it's OK to do it and then there is something about being in - this - thing - together that helps us to be close. Intimacy, then, becomes a constant and we can focus on other areas of our lives.

Two, intimacy can grow with time. Two people who have been together for 20 years can have a deeper connection than they did when they had only been dating for three months. (Of course, time together doesn't insure intimacy but it does make a space for that to happen)

It takes time for us to know each other. As trust builds, we open ourselves; and over the months (or years) we reveal ourselves. Also, people tend to change; if we keep

*It's not intimacy we fear,
but the price we think we'll
have to pay for it.*

our closeness through years of changes, we know more about each other than anyone else and our contact is deep indeed.

Conversely, the intimacy that comes with coupling is also one of the problems that people in couples experience. Couples often feel stress about too much intimacy—not enough separateness.

Many of us are afraid of closeness because we believe that we'll have to stay there forever, or that our partner will feel hurt if we pull away. Some of us believe that closeness carries obligations to always please, or take care of, or be taken care of, or never change our mind.

Each person has their own particular scare about intimacy and IT'S IMPORTANT TO NOTE THAT WE AREN'T SCARED OF INTIMACY ITSELF, BUT THE CONSEQUENCES THAT WE BELIEVE GO ALONG WITH IT.

Often, because of this mixed desire of wanting intimacy and fearing it, we put up barriers. Out of our awareness we invite closeness and push it away at the same time. Or we get close to our partner and then push away in a hurtful way because we don't know that it's OK to take whatever distance or closeness we need.

If we let ourselves look past the scare to our wants, we discover that we have a natural flow from separateness to contact to merging and back again . . .

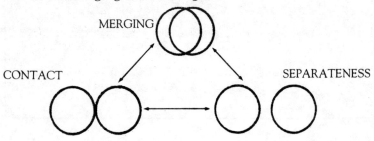

Merging is focusing intensely on each other. Contact is being together, focusing on some other thing. Separateness is being apart, focusing on different things.

I think it's easier to understand this natural flow process when observing children. Little Sally comes to Daddy's lap for attention. She makes contact, distracts him from reading, and he picks her up. For a while they merge, with Sally snuggled in Daddy's lap for a quiet conversation. Then Sally begins to fidget, Daddy soon puts her down, and she runs off to play, knowing he'll be there when she wants to be close again. In the meantime, she may ask an occasional question, or say "Look, Daddy" at what she is doing. This provides contact, and reassures her of his availability.

A couple, too, will go through the same stages. Bill comes home harassed by his day, so Jane fixes a cool drink or a cup of coffee and leaves him alone. After half an hour, he wanders into the kitchen, asking "What's for dinner?" Then Jane, seeing an opportunity for contact, has options. She can get sexy and suggest herself as an appetizer, or ask Bill to sit down and tell her about his day, or simply say "roast beef" and let him decide about their degree of contact at the moment. Knowing there's a flow and that no stage is permanent allows her to give him the "space" he needs, and also to ask for what she wants. He gets his turn to initiate or respond to contact equally often.

Learning to recognize the stages of that flow enables us to relax and enjoy them instead of hanging on or backing off. For example, when I am making contact with you after being separate, I will know that this is our "contact stage" and I can enjoy it without constant pushing to be closer. I won't need to push because I know that, with us, contact leads to merging.

Also, when we're very close and intense, I can recognize this as our "merging stage." Knowing that we will eventually separate again, I won't be afraid that I'll never get time to myself.

So, once a loving relationship is begun, it is important to find that natural flow between contact, merging and separateness.

In the next section, we'll look at some of the barriers to that flow, then move on to learn how to find the flow once the barriers are known.

SECTION II

THE BARRIERS

A PROBLEM:

Philburt is in New York City and wants to be in Key West. No matter how much Philburt dreams of Key West and yearns for Key West, he is still in New York City. The more he hates New York and denies he's in New York, the more likely he is to remain.

However, once Philburt says, "I'm in New York. Now how do I get to Key West?" he's on his way. Once he acknowledges that he's in New York, he can figure out how to get to Grand Central Station or Kennedy Airport to buy a ticket to Key West. If Philburt doesn't know he's in New York or doesn't face the fact that he's in New York, he's powerless to move, and *pretending* to be in Key West just doesn't do the job.

This section, "The Barriers," is about New York City. (Section I is about Key West and Section III is how to get there from here.)

Reading about our barriers can be unpleasant, although it needn't be. Remember that everyone has them more or less and that we *can* leave them behind. Barriers, like any problems, are simply mechanisms for learning. Approaching your barriers as challenges, rather than tragedies, and dealing with them accordingly can give you a tremendous feeling of satisfaction and competence.

If exploring your barriers becomes oppressive, remind yourself that awareness is power for making changes—

whatever changes you want. Rejoice at your new awareness. Also feel free to skip over to the "How To" section to
reassure yourself that there *is* a way out.

*Seeing barriers as challenges
and overcoming them
can give you a tremendous feeling
of satisfaction and competence.*

CHAPTER 3

HOW WE SHOULD – OUGHTA– HAFTA BE

We live with a network of invisible beliefs and rules which tell us how to think, feel and act in order to be acceptable (loved). These rules are usually invisible because they masquerade as facts (i.e., women aren't logical and men aren't intuitive). Since most of us follow these rules, more or less, we can take surveys and establish "scientifically" that most women aren't logical and most men aren't intuitive. What we don't see clearly is that women can be as logical as men if they will allow themselves to risk being unacceptable, begin thinking logically and practice it. Likewise, men can risk being intuitive if they will let themselves feel feelings and listen to their inner voice instead of ignoring it.

A necessary first step to coupling as free individuals, then, is to look clearly at the invisible rules and beliefs we are following. When we are clear about these rules and beliefs, then we can find the ones we like and reaffirm them and replace the ones we don't like with new beliefs that allow us intimacy *and* freedom.

Here is a partial list of rules that create the *majority cultural stereotype* in the USA. There are variations within minority cultures and between individuals. We suggest that you use these examples as a starting place for finding out your own rules.

SOME TRADITIONAL RULES FOR BEING

A MAN...	A WOMAN...
is logical.	is intuitive.
doesn't feel feelings.	feels feelings.
doesn't cry.	is emotional.
doesn't nurture.	is nurturing.
does for himself.	does for others.
is assertive (yang).	is receptive (yin).
is powerful.	is powerless.
is aggressive.	is passive.
is independent.	is dependent.
loves conditionally.	loves unconditionally.
is insensitive and hard.	is sensitive and soft.
is effective.	is ineffective.
is sexually aggressive.	acts and looks sexy, but doesn't enjoy sex.
is overt and direct.	is covert and manipulative.
loves awkwardly, holds back expressing.	loves easily.
feels angry, not scared.	feels scared or sad, not angry.

In the last few years, through the women's movement and the humanist movement, these rules have begun to change. The greatest change so far is with the women's rules which limit power. Women are beginning to receive cultural endorsement for being powerful, effective and enjoying sex. To a lesser extent, men are getting endorsement for feeling feelings and being nurturing, sensitive and intuitive.

*Hogamus higamus
men are polygamous;
higamus hogamus
women monogamous.*

—traditional rule
via Dorothy Parker

SOME TRADITIONAL RULES
FOR BEING SINGLE

A SINGLE MAN . . .
is independent.
doesn't need others.
is an adventurer.
is lonely.
is a Don Juan.
feels in danger of being
    trapped.
is carefree.
is irresponsible.
is not fully mature.
won't *really* be happy till
    he finds a woman.

A SINGLE WOMAN . . .
is unlovable.
is hard.
is an old maid.
is lonely.
wants to be a man.
is not fulfilled.
is looking for a man.
won't *really* be happy till
    she finds a man.

Here, too, the rules and beliefs are slowly changing so that
a woman who is free and single gets credit for being adventurous, independent and lovable.

SOME TRADITIONAL RULES FOR
BEING IN A COUPLE

A MAN . . .
(dating)
initiates contact.
makes decisions.
pays for entertainment.

(cohabitating and/or
    married)
earns the money

A WOMAN . . .
(dating)
has veto power.
manipulates.

(cohabitating and/or
    married)
saves the money
spends the money
keeps house (or works *and*
    keeps house.)

A MAN . . .	A WOMAN . . .
mostly does what *he* likes.	mostly does what *they* like.
goes out with the boys.	stays home.
	works on the relationship (more women will read this book than men).
is sexually promiscuous.	is sexually monogamous.
is responsible to the world.	is responsible to the family. (her relatives *and* his).
protects family from the outside world.	supports and validates the men.
	preserves the culture (in charge of family cultural and aesthetic activities).

These rules seem to have changed much less than the ones for individual men and women outside the couple relationship (hence, this book).

A NECESSARY DIGRESSION

By now, you've no doubt noticed how restrictive these rules are.

Women began to notice their oppression under these rules some time back, got angry and began to do something about changing them. Part of the reason they noticed is connected to their cultural permission to feel feelings. Because they could feel their stress, they knew that there was a problem before the men did. They took a long time to act because of cultural sanctions against feminine assertiveness, but they did act and are still acting.

Men have been slower to notice their oppression under these rules. (One example of that oppression: the stress of maintaining an artificial one-up position plus the stress of suppressing feelings probably often leads to early death from degenerative diseases.) Because men are not supposed to acknowledge feelings, they are enjoined from knowing that there is stress. Fortunately, some women are so assertive that they're impossible to ignore, and men are beginning to recognize (if not feel) that there is, indeed, a problem.

The point is that we need not be slaves to these rules.

Begin to notice (if you haven't already) how these rules and beliefs restrict people. Because noticing is the beginning of power to do something about it for yourself and others. We *can* do something about it. Some people (including you) have already begun.

We are not powerless.

End of digression.

TRADITIONAL RULES FOR COUPLES (AS A UNIT)

People in couples are socially acceptable.
They become *one.*
They own each other (in some cultures the man owns the
    woman).
They have mutual interests.
They have more power together than they both had
    separately.
They are responsible for and to each other.
Their individual interests are subordinate to their
    common interest.
They ask each other's permission.
They own everything in common.
Sex is fantastic every time.

Frequency of sex decreases with time.
They have intimate contact only with each other.
They present a harmonious front.
If married, they will have children.
They only socialize with other couples.
They live happily ever after.

These rules have begun to change recently. In some social circles it's OK not to have kids if the couple is married. Divorce is acceptable in some groups. A few marriages are open in terms of intimate contact with others. Some couples are experimenting with variations of these rules in an effort to free up their relationships.

In Chapter 2, we mentioned cultural reasons for coupling. Now that we've looked at some of the cultural rules about how to be, we can see that they exert a lot of pressure for people to couple up. According to the cultural rules, single people have less power and less acceptability than couples.

Full-fledged adulthood comes with marriage.

Intimacy outside of a couple relationship is suspect and inside the relationship it is guaranteed (Two Become One).

Happiness is only available as a couple.

That couples have more social power and acceptability within the majority culture is a fact. Beyond that, the intimacy and happiness promised do not happen automatically and are, in fact, extremely unlikely considering that the partners have so restricted themselves to fit a cultural mold. The idea of being happy while not being yourself is suspect. If I must distrust and deny myself in order to be acceptable to others, then my happiness is as restricted as I am.

RULES, BELIEFS AND PERMISSION

There *are* times to follow the rules.

Before going on to alternatives, it's important to note that having rules to follow can sometimes take the pressure off. If I meet someone new, and I know the rules of etiquette, I can relax to some degree. I am following guidelines we *both* know, and my new friend will not be shocked or disgusted or otherwise "turned off" by my behavior. We have a chance to get to know each other and *then* relax the rules a bit. If I wish to be accepted by a group of people too large to know well as individuals, I can accomplish that by learning the rules of the group and following them. Public relations teams are experts at discovering the rules for a person or company to follow in order to be accepted by the people. The candidate or company that convinces the people most thoroughly, wins.

So, sometimes following the rules is desirable.

Also note that some of the specific rules and beliefs are *very* desirable. For instance, most men would not be willing to give up their thinking ability, nor would most women want to give up their intuition.

The problem is that these are *rules* and are, therefore, *required* for acceptability. If a woman chooses to subordinate her feelings to her ability to think, she's culturally unacceptable, not only because she thinks well, but because she isn't sensitive to her feelings.

What we recommend is turning the desired rules into permission and revising the belief. "Permission" is using the rule as a possible alternative, yet not rigidly enforcing it, or making it the *only* alternative.

For example:

Rule: A man must be logical (If he isn't logical, he isn't a man).

Permission: It's OK for a man to be logical if and when he wants (it's also OK for a man to be illogical or intuitive).

New Belief: *All* people are capable of logical thought.

Rule: A woman must be nurturing and take care of people (if she doesn't, she isn't a woman).

Permission: It's OK for a woman to nurture and take care of people if and when she wants (it's also OK for her to decline OR to be nurtured and taken care of).

New Belief: *All* people are capable of nurturing and taking care of people.

ULTIMATELY EACH PERSON WILL DECIDE FOR ONESELF WHICH RULES TO KEEP (AND TURN INTO PERMISSION) AND WHICH TO IGNORE.

SUGGESTIONS FOR DISCOVERING YOUR OWN SECRET (OR NOT-SO-SECRET) RULES:

1. Use the lists in this chapter as a checklist. Check the items which you think apply to you and your relationship(s).

Make your own list wherever your rules are different. One way to get started would be to make lists under the headings:

My Mom's Rules for Being a Man.
My Mom's Rules for Being a Woman.
My Dad's Rules for Being a Woman.
My Dad's Rules for Being a Man.
My Family's Rules for Being a Couple.

As you do this, you may hear the voice of a parent or family member in your head, saying, "Big Boys Don't

We each define our own restrictions.

That's freedom.

Cry," or some other rule. Once you get started, the rules will come out easily.

One of the things that keeps these rules in effect is secrecy about what they are, so we all have some blocks to knowing the rules. Going back to the original source (Mom and Dad, teachers, TV, etc.) can help. So can a quiet period of rest. Sitting quietly, not struggling for the rules but simply letting yourself know that there *are* rules, may be just the space you need for discovery. Remember to do it at *your* pace. You already may have been pondering the restrictions on your life for a while; if so, this will come very easily. Or, it may be a totally new concept which you need to live with for a few minutes, hours or days before the list begins to grow. If the latter situation is yours, try keeping the idea of "cultural rules" and "role-playing" in mind during your daily activities.

You'll soon begin seeing examples in the people around you, and then in yourself. Write these down and you have your list. Don't be discouraged if it goes slowly at first. It often does.

As you make your list, you'll probably discover some of your partner's rules. This knowledge can be helpful for *you* in looking at *your* couples rules. Don't share your discovery until you've made *sure* he or she is interested and wants to hear it. If you don't, your discovery will probably be neither heard nor appreciated.

Remember, the process is intended to allow *you* freedom from your own rules. Your partner may not want more freedom than he or she has. The same thing goes for friends, coworkers, relatives, parents and children. If you find that this process is as good for you as we believe it is, your partner, friends, relatives, etc., will notice. If you have not already irritated them with "preaching" about your newfound freedom, they'll begin to ask how you made the change. *Then* is the time to tell them.

If you already have clear communication with your partner or a close friend or relative, you may bring up the subject casually—or even with excitement. The point is to be sure the other person *wants* to hear about it. It is not up to you to "fix" his or her life, just as it is not anyone else's responsibility to fix yours.

2. Once you have a list, you can begin to look at the things you like and the things you don't like.

At this point in the process, it's very important to think about and experience what you like and don't like on the list with equal emphasis.

It is important *not* to think, just yet, about *changing* the things you don't like. Stay with the knowledge, live with your new awareness for days, weeks, or even months, if you like. Don't hassle yourself about your new knowledge. CONGRATULATE YOURSELF ON YOUR DIS-COVERY.

If you're quite uncomfortable with certain things in your life, this can be a difficult place to go slow. When we first begin to see the root of a problem, we have a tendency to try to destroy it immediately. Keep in mind that success does not come with *stopping* a process, because that leaves a gap to be filled. Therefore, either the old process will come back into the empty space, or something else unintentional will. What we propose is *replacing* the old process with a new process chosen by you. This leaves no gaps and is highly successful. It also takes time.

Our favorite illustration about the difference between *stopping* a process and *replacing* a process is the "elephant" example. Try *not* thinking about elephants. See? Now try

*D*o not
think of
an elephant.

(Lots of luck.)

thinking about camels instead. It suddenly becomes possible to replace the elephants. Behavior and beliefs work the same way.

The point is to replace the old, undesirable behavior or belief each time it occurs. Quitting smoking is a good example of how this works. Many of the successful stop smoking programs focus on replacing old smoking habits with new behavior. The old habits are like the elephants and the new behavior is like the camels in the previous example.

This is also a matter of focus. As a general rule, we reinforce any behavior we focus attention on. It does not matter whether the attention is negative or positive. If I bite my fingernails and I want to stop, I can attempt to stop by telling myself it's bad, I'll have ugly hands, etc. When I realize my fingers are in my mouth, I can take them out again and tell myself how bad the habit is. All the time I'm doing that and struggling with the urge to bite, I'm focusing on the fact that biting my nails is important to me. However, if when I realize my fingers are in my mouth, I immediately do something like needlepoint that keeps my hands busy and I pop a hard candy in my mouth, I am replacing the behavior with more enjoyable pastimes, and the nailbiting does not get stronger. If I then get into the habit of going for a manicure weekly, I suddenly have a reason to take pride in how well my hands look. I have now replaced the need to keep my hands and mouth busy with more enjoyable habits, and I have given myself a reason to feel good where I felt bad before. There is no longer any benefit to the old habit and it will die quite easily.

So, for now, be a scientist. Examine your behavior and conditions as though you were making a scientific study.

Scientists do not change the process which happens in experiments. They simply observe and record. To change is to invalidate the experiment and create a new one in midstream.

Congratulate yourself on being an aware person. Look at this as the first step in creating the life *you* want. The more thoroughly this first step is done, the better the result.

The process of making the changes that you want to make comes later and will be described in due time.

CHAPTER 4

COMPETITION & WANTING

People want.
We're made that way.
People want love.
> comfort.
> ice cream.
> money.
> shoes.
> food.
> attention.
> fun.
> success.
> a puppy.
> power.
> whatever.

And we're taught we're *not* supposed to want.

We're also taught, most of us, that there isn't enough for everyone and we have to compete with others to get enough. Enough food. Enough fun. Enough money. Enough love. Enough of whatever it is that we want.

Competition makes us better people, we are told.
Survival of the fittest.
Maybe that was true once. Maybe.

It's not true now.
There IS enough to go around.

But, since we believe that there isn't, we compete with each other, and the "winners" stockpile it (food, money, love or whatever) and the "losers" don't have enough. The result is that we see all those millions of folks who don't have enough and we think that that proves there isn't enough to go around.

As part of our basic training for survival in a competitive world, most of us are taught to curb our wants. (A few of us are taught to go for what we want and that in order to get it we will be depriving someone else. These few are the "successful" people. Their *traditional stereotype* is cold, unfeeling, rich and basically unhappy, because the wealth has been gained at the expense of depriving others.)

Most of us are taught NOT to want from early infancy.
We are told:
> We shouldn't want what we want.
> We'll never get exactly what we want.
> We shouldn't ask for what we want.
> Asking is demanding.
> We should get what we want without asking. If we have to ask, then getting it doesn't count.
> Nice girls and boys don't ask—they wait until it is offered.
> Other people's wants are more important than ours.
> If we get what we want others will be deprived.
> Don't say no to a request.
> Be generous, give away what you have (share).
> Wanting is selfish.
> Wanting is greedy.

How did you feel when you read the "being free" definitions in Chapter 1 of Section I? When we read that list in

There is enough
to go around.

our class, the reaction is often defensive. Our students are disbelieving, hostile, antagonistic. We sometimes get into several class sessions of "What if's" (e.g.: What if your partner wants to eat at 6:00 and you don't? What if all your friends call you selfish? What if your partner winds up doing all the giving, and you do all the getting? What if you want to be with someone who wants other things?). We hope to answer some of these questions as we go along, and we especially hope that you'll discover the means to answer your own "what if's" as they happen.

The point is that we are taught that satisfying ourselves is wrong and means someone else will have to be deprived. That is another way of saying there's not enough to go around. Generally, in our class, the women have been afraid that if they say what they want, no one will love them and they won't get it anyway. Also, they felt that if the men ask for what they want, the women will wind up doing all the giving and never get. In short, they believed that there is no straightforward way for women to get what they want.

Often, the men felt that they were supposed to be strong and not need things. Wanting was "sissyish" and proved that they were not real men. Oriental and Jewish men particularly (a result of cultural rules) felt they couldn't have what they wanted anyway. So, to save themselves pain, they learned not to know that they have wants.

Since we do have wants and we're taught not to, we're in a bind. So, we learn to fake it, each in our own way. Some of us pretend we don't want, even to the point of not knowing consciously that we want. Some of us have an internal argument between our "wanting self" and our "self that enforces the rules" and stay confused about what we want. Some of us look for someone else who will furnish our wants for us. (There are couples who get together in order to take care of each other because it's not OK for each to take care of oneself.)

Regardless of how we decide to fake it, we invariably end up not getting what we want and feeling dissatisfied without knowing why. This happens because we simply cannot get what we want with any regularity unless we acknowledge our wants and feel OK about satisfying them.

Here's an example of that:
Tom: "What do you want to do tonight?"
Gerry: "I don't know, Tom, what do you want to do?"
This leads to the feeling that "we never have anything to do."

If Tom were in touch with his wants he could say something more specific, like: "I've been working hard all week, my job is dull, and I'd like some excitement tonight. I've been thinking about going out for cocktails and dinner at a fancy restaurant so I could get dressed up. Do you want to do that?"

Then, if Gerry is in touch with her wants, she might say, "Gee, I've been in this business suit and out to fancy lunches all week—what I'd like to do is watch sports on TV with you beside me."

From there, they can negotiate toward a mutual decision —perhaps going out to a sports event which would be comfortable for Gerry and exciting for Tom—or perhaps cooking a fancy meal together which they could dress up for and then watch TV after, or inviting friends over for dinner, with TV after.

So, knowing what I want and saying (not demanding) what I want are part of being free and essential to people working together to be free in their relationship. There-

Wanting
comes first.

Getting
comes second.

fore, our indoctrination about wanting and competing are barriers indeed.

When we (Tina and Riley) say that we can work together to solve conflicts so that we *both* get *exactly* what we want, we're usually not believed!

Section III contains instructions for working together to solve conflicts so that everyone gets exactly what one wants.

The process only works if each person involved is willing and able to say 100% of what one wants. For most of us, identifying our wants violates some very deeply held early training.

SO, WHAT'S TO DO?

First, separate wanting from getting.
Wanting is a different thing from getting.
Wanting doesn't require thinking or action, it just is.
Getting requires thinking and action.
Wanting comes first.
Getting comes second.
It is OK to know a want and not have it fulfilled. And at the same time, knowing a want is prerequisite to having it filled. So wanting clearly comes first, whether it is to be fulfilled or not.

This chapter is on wanting.
Getting (without depriving others) comes later.
Second, get acquainted with wanting—and practice.
Start simple.
Hold your breath and then notice when you want to take a breath.

The next time you're hungry, stop. Let yourself be quiet for a few moments and notice what you want to eat. Imagine a smorgasbord passing before your eyes and notice which items are most appealing to you (sometimes people notice that what they want is different from what they thought they wanted!).

One way to get acquainted with wanting is with a childlike fantasy which goes like this:

Think of yourself as about seven years old, or an age that for you is fun and free.

Imagine that you are in a comfortable pleasant place (i.e., your bedroom, playhouse, a meadow, the attic) enjoying being alone there.

Imagine that a kindly wizard appears and offers to give you anything and everything you want. The *only* restriction is that you must write them down and you have exactly ten minutes in which to do it. YOU CAN HAVE EVERY-THING THAT YOU CAN WRITE DOWN IN TEN MINUTES. He hands you paper and pen and you begin.

In imagining this fantasy, it is important to impose no limitations on your wants. They can be child wants or grown-up wants or both. Don't edit them just because they don't seem feasible, seem contradictory, or might impose on someone.

Another way to discover a want is to start with a "don't want."

Since our prohibition about wanting usually leaves us dissatisfied, we often have easy access to what we DON'T want.

Here's a way to change a "don't want" into a "do want."

Sara decides that she doesn't want to do all the housework anymore.

"Don't want" is a backward way of saying "want." It usually indicates that there is something I want that I'm not getting. The problem with "don't want" is that it doesn't lead to alternatives in negotiating. In order to negotiate alternatives, Sara needs to discover the "want" behind the "don't want."

So, Sara looks at housekeeping and her thoughts and feelings about it:
Sometimes she enjoys cleaning house or straightening up the place.
Usually she doesn't.
And now that she realizes it's not a natural law that women do housework, she likes it even less.

At this point she tends to get confused with conflicting ideas:
Her partner wouldn't do housework for anything—he'll laugh at her if she asks him to help.
He might be mad (or scared?).
He'll say OK and then not do it.
If *she* doesn't do it, it won't get done.
She likes the place neat and he doesn't care, so why should he help?
She's stuck with the job.
There's no hope.
She feels angry or scared or sad or all three.

The confusion comes from thinking up solutions before being clear about what she wants in place of what she doesn't want. So, she makes a list (without editing) of what she does want:

1. I want to do half of the housework.

2. I don't want to do any housework.
3. I want to push a button and have the house clean itself.
4. I want him to do half the housework.
5. I want him to do all the housework.
6. I want to share the responsibility for housecleaning with him on an equal basis.
7. I want to move to a clean house every week.
8. I don't mind housecleaning, but I want to be recognized for doing it in the same way he would if he did it.
9. I don't mind housecleaning, but I want him to cooperate by picking up his stuff and cleaning up his messes.
10. I want to live in a house that's ____% neat ____% of the time.
11. I want someone besides me to clean my house.

Chances are one or more of these wants will apply. Note that #1 is more of a solution than a want compared to #3, #6, #8, #10 or #11. Number 2 is a "don't want" and therefore not useful at this stage. Numbers 4, 5 and 9 are wants for him and more solutions than wants. Numbers 3 and 7 are "off the wall" when viewed critically, but they are the kinds of wants that are bound to show up in an unedited want-list. They are clear and childlike and indicate that the search for wants is an honest one. Enjoy them. Let's say that #6 is the want that "feels best" to her. "I want to share the responsibility for housecleaning with him on an equal basis."

In discussing solutions, she needs to be clear what housecleaning amounts to, so she can add #10, "I want the house to be 90% neat 70% of the time." Some examples of that will probably help her to be clear:
Messy in the mornings is OK.
I want neatness in the living room and bedroom mostly when I'm at home, the kitchen when I start cooking, and the front rooms and yard when we have company, etc.

Once she feels clear with herself, she is ready to negotiate.

At this point it will be necessary for her partner to go through a similar process to clarify his wants about house-keeping in order to proceed with the negotiating process.

Some people who want to get acquainted with wanting (and some who are old hands) keep a Want List and add to it as they think of new things—it's fun to do, and provides an easy solution to the times when you "can't think of anything to do."

A Want List might look like this:

THINGS TO DO FOR FUN:

RESTAURANTS:
casual   fancy
  Jojo's   The Ritz
  The Rat Race   Chasen's

AMUSEMENTS:
  bowling
  ice skating
  make bread-dough sculptures
  horseback riding
  look through the old trunk in the attic
  etc.

THINGS I WANT:
  inflatable raft
  golf shoes
  etc.

So, practice wanting.
Have fun.

Don't let feasibility or practicality get in the way.
Brainstorm.
Get ridiculous.
Don't go for what you want yet.
Don't implement your wants,
just practice wanting for now:

I want $10,000 per month from now on.
      a red cowboy shirt.
      to be famous and loved by millions.
      a Sopwith Camel.
      _____ to take me to dinner tonight.
      to be eight feet tall.
      a banana split.
      to be massaged after a steam bath.
      a ten-speed bike.
      ten new friends this month.
      sex with Robert Redford.
      a two-week vacation away from the kids.
      etc.

*H*ave
fun.

CHAPTER 5

LOW SELF ESTEEM AND FEAR OF LONELINESS

Everyone is worthwhile (and lovable).

Everyone I know questions their worth.

Some do it very seldom, some do it often.

Generally people who usually feel worthy began life in an environment (a family) where they were loved and validated often. Their ideas were heard, their feelings respected and they saw themselves as effective in making things happen.

At the other extreme, the people who usually feel worthless began life in an environment where they were not wanted, were ignored (or mistreated) and saw themselves as helpless in making things happen.

In the middle are most of us who had some of both extremes in our early lives and know both feelings of worth *and* worthlessness.

IMPORTANT: Our early environment has no effect whatever on whether we are worthwhile or not, lovable or not. We may *act* worthless because we feel worthless. We may *act* unlovable because we *feel* unlovable. But underneath our actions, we *are* worthwhile. We *are* lovable. Period.

Our early environment effects whether we are *aware* of our worth or not. And further, just because our early environment led us to believe that we are unworthy and unlovable, this doesn't mean we can't change our mind about it. We can. Neither does it mean that we aren't responsible for what we do. We are.

Now, let's look at a couple relationship built out of feelings of worthlessness.

If I feel worthless, I also feel unlovable, and the only way anyone will ever be interested in me, the only way anyone will ever love me, is if I fake being worthy and lovable. Then they will love the fake me and the real me remains unloved. So, the most I can ever hope for is to rip off love and affection from my "friends;" that is, to be loved for being "someone else."

Another thing I can do is to get someone involved in a "committed" relationship—like, get married "till death do us part." That's pretty easy because I can fake being lovable and worthy during the courtship period and then after the wedding I can relax and be the "real" worthless me.

This is not as easy as it once was. When divorce was a terrible sin, it meant social ostracism. No one would dare socialize with someone who had initiated a divorce, because they were automatically "adulterers." Therefore, couples stayed together no matter what; so if an "unworthy" person managed to get married, one had it made. Today, however, divorce has been made relatively simple. Consequently, despite vows and ceremonies, people do

*E*veryone
is
lovable.

Period.

not feel as irrevocably obligated as they once did. So if I let down my guard, my partner may find someone who looks more lovable than I do and leave.

So, I'd better find a partner who feels worthless, too. Because then both of us will stay with each other out of fear that we'll never find anyone else dumb enough to commit themselves to us.

Freedom will be out of the question for me because I'm not worthy of wanting what I want or getting what I want and my early experience is that if I go for what I want, I won't be loved.

In order to be loved, I must put all my energy into fulfilling my partner's wants, not mine—doing a lot of mind-reading because saying wants is not allowed. Incidentally, I'll expect my partner to take care of my wants, not hers (or his) and if she (or he) doesn't, I'll be angry (or hurt) and thereby prove I'm unworthy or unlovable.

So, our couple relationship is a form of bondage enforced by our assumption that if we part, we will be unloved.

Now, let's look at a couple relationship built out of feelings of worth.

I feel worthwhile and lovable. The way for me to be loved is to be myself. The way to be myself is to validate my ideas, wants and feelings.

Since one of my most important wants is to love and be loved, I'll be on the lookout for worthwhile and lovable friends who want to love me.

I will couple up with a partner who feels worthwhile and lovable. Someone whose wants include me being who I am.

We will get together because it feels good to be together, because we both get what we want—each of us knowing that if we part, we will not go unloved.

Because we are open and honest with each other, we each feel truly loved for who we really are. Being together is easy and unpressured, since we are being ourselves, with no faking. As time goes on, we develop more and more trust and closeness. After a short time, we have a solid history of trust, closeness and good feelings which makes us extremely valuable to each other.

The force that keeps us together is a mutual commitment to feeling good together and getting what we want together, plus the mutual knowledge that feeling good is easy in this relationship.

The fact is, that most of us feel worthy at times and unworthy at times, and our relationships have elements of both.

Since feeling worthy and lovable in a relationship is *not* a barrier to a free couple relationship, and since feeling worthless and unlovable *is*, it is important for the partners to figure out how to survive those troubled times.

First, don't fight it. Accept the feelings and put them out in the open: "I feel ugly and unlovable right now and I can't even figure out why you're still here."

Second, decide whether you want to be alone for a while with your partner or with a friend outside the couple. Don't be with your partner if you're irritating each other. There are times to be separate and times to be together, and if you accept that as true, you'll be able to figure out which one is right for now.

Third, don't try to solve problems with your partner until you find your "lovableness" again.

Fourth, if worthless and unlovable is a regular feeling for you, or if you keep yourself out of satisfying relationships because of it, you might want to find a good counselor or psychotherapist to help you find your lovable, worthy self.

Your partner probably can't help you find your worthy, lovable self. He or she probably has problems that relate to your worthless feelings and lacks the objectivity of a trained counselor or therapist.

So, while your partner can love and support you, a counselor or therapist is the one who can help you make needed changes.

CHAPTER 6

SECRET AGREEMENTS

Often people have agreements that they aren't aware of.

Sometimes these agreements are basic to their relationship, and both partners are invested in not knowing about them.

Here is an example of this type of agreement:

She says: "Make me stay home because I'm scared about going out and dealing with people and I don't want to admit I'm scared."

He agrees: "I'll make you stay home so that I'll be reassured that you'll always be there when I need you."

There are usually other sub-agreements connected to this agreement. For instance:

Her: "Make me stay home and thereby prove that men are possessive and cruel."

Him: "Be scared to go out and thereby prove that women are dependent and incompetent."

People who have low self-esteem and feel worthless and unlovable commonly make agreements like this. Because their relationship is based on this agreement, there is a chance that discovering their lovableness could end their reasons for being a couple. They might take a look at their hidden agreement, laugh (or get angry) and say goodbye.

On the other hand, finding their worth and lovableness will more likely add greater warmth, excitement and intimacy to their relationship. Bringing the secrets out into the open can free them from old, boring patterns. Once the secret agreements are exposed, people have the power to negotiate new agreements which allow each of them more freedom. With more freedom, they experience more self-esteem and feel more lovable.

Put yourself in this spot for a while. If you and I were a couple, and you knew I felt free to leave at any time, and I were with you, then you'd know I *want* to be here. After all, it's not something I have to do, so if I wanted to be somewhere else, I would be. Do you feel the compliment in that? You would automatically be someone I want to be with, someone I enjoy—just by the fact of my being here. And I would get the same compliment from your presence. After a while, these good feelings would fill a large percentage of our time. We would both feel worthwhile.

When a couple has secret agreements like our example, they usually need outside help to sort them out—help sorting out their agreements, and help discovering their worth.

Many secret agreements are closer to the surface and easier to deal with. Here's an example:

Him: "I'll show I love you by having dinner on the table every night at 6:30, and you show you love me by being home every night at 6:00."

Her: "I'll show I love you by being home at 6:00 and you show you love me by having dinner on at 6:30."

What happens with this kind of agreement is that if either partner is late or doesn't show up, the reaction is usually all out of proportion to the circumstances—at least it seems out of proportion, unless we realize that the issue is really whether they love each other or not. According to the secret agreement, "If you are late, that means you don't love me," and/or "If dinner isn't ready on time, you don't love me."

If this agreement were out in the open, the reaction would be understood and the partners would probably renegotiate the agreement so that there were alternate ways of demonstrating their love and alternatives about arriving home and fixing dinner. The issue of arriving home and dinner would be clearly separated from the issue of demonstrating love.

Sometimes the partners think they have agreements when they really don't:

Her: "I'll do the dishes and you do the cooking." ·

Him: "I'll do the cooking and you maintain the car."

Because this agreement is unspoken, the partner who is diligently doing the dishes may find herself in the dog house when the car breaks down and not know why.

A secret agreement isn't a problem unless it's broken. Then there are bad feelings and nobody knows exactly what the bad feelings are about.

A secret agreement is a barrier *only* because it is secret. Its power to disrupt disappears when it is out in the open, because then it can either be consciously followed or changed.

If Betty knows for certain that Tom sees her cooking as an expression of her love, (she can *only* know for certain if they've talked about it. Guesses, intuitions, and familiarity are not really certain) then, when she comes up unwilling, uneager or unable to cook one day, she can make sure Tom knows she loves him by saying so, or demonstrating it another way, and thus avoid an upsetting reaction.

So, the next process we wish to discuss is locating and clarifying secret agreements.

DISCOVERING SECRET AGREEMENTS

In a sense, a secret agreement is a two-sided expectation. Each partner expects the other to behave a certain way. As long as these expectations are met, the agreement will be secret.

It is very difficult to uncover our expectations because we take them for granted. As a result, the best and easiest way to discover a secret agreement is to wait for it to be broken. If I notice that I'm surprised at your action or words and then experience a feeling of being betrayed, I can suspect a secret agreement. We all have a favorite feeling that we feel when we think we've been betrayed. Some of us feel angry, some sad, or hurt, or scared. If I feel that feeling, and it seems to be more intense than the circumstances justify, then there's a very good chance that I've discovered a secret agreement.

For example: We've been together five years and you have always cleaned up after me—picked up my clothes, washed my dirty dishes, apologized when I missed appointments, etc. One day I come home and my clothes are still strewn around. I check to see if you're sick, and I find a note saying you went to lunch with a friend. I feel scared and confused—I'm very upset.

Since you left a note, I have no reason to think you've been kidnapped, in an accident, etc. And my reaction is larger than the mild annoyance or sense of discomfort a disorderly house should produce. So I know there's a secret agreement violation.

Once I suspect a secret agreement, I need to verbalize my expectation to myself and then ask myself what my side of the bargain should be. If, for instance, you're late for dinner and I feel betrayed and hurt, I can look at my expectation about that: "I expect you to be home at 6:30—you're always home at 6:30, and I fix dinner so that it's ready when you get home. I do that out of my love for you and I want you to know that. I feel reassured when you come home at 6:30—I know you love me because you always come home." So, it looks like my side of the secret agreement is, "I show I love you by having dinner on at 6:30 and you show you love me by being home by 6:30." Now, I can check with my partner to see if there's a secret agreement on her side.

Whether my partner is involved in the secret agreement or not, we can still negotiate an overt agreement about demonstrating our love, arrival times and dinner.

*I'm in charge
of what I feel
and do.
Just me.
Nobody else.*

CHAPTER 7

WHO'S IN CHARGE HERE?

"You make me mad!"

"He really knows how to push my button."

"She finally hooked me into her game."

"I can't have fun if you're in a sulk."

One of the important barriers to freedom in any relationship is confusion about who is responsible for our feelings and actions.

EACH OF US IS COMPLETELY IN CHARGE OF OUR OWN FEELINGS AND ACTIONS AND NO ONE ELSE'S.

Most people find this difficult to accept because our decisions about feeling and acting are usually automatic and out of our awareness. In addition, there is general agreement in our culture that we are not in charge. This is most obvious in the soap operas. If all the characters on *As the World Turns* were to recognize their responsibility for their own lives, the program would no longer have a premise.

Denying our responsibility for ourselves is great for melodrama, but wreaks havoc with being free in our relationships.

Darlene: Damn, you make me mad! Everytime I try to
            relax and have some fun playing my guitar, you
            huff out of the room or try to talk to me. I've
            quit playing because you don't like it. I'm finally
            fed up!

Rosa: Well, you leave me out when you play and sing.
            Nobody likes to be left out.

Darlene: It's not my fault that you won't join in.

Rosa: I can't help it if I'm tone deaf.

Darlene: Look, just because you don't enjoy music
            doesn't mean you can keep me from enjoying it.
            That's what makes me so mad—you won't let
            me enjoy it!

Rosa and Darlene share the belief that Darlene's singing
and playing make Rosa feel left out and that Rosa's resentment (or scare) keeps Darlene from enjoying singing and
playing. They've each placed their well being in the hands
of the other and are in a hopeless struggle to make the
other act differently so that they can each feel good.

Now, let's see what happens if they take responsibility for
their feelings and actions.

Darlene: Damn, I'm mad! Everytime I try to relax and
            have some fun playing my guitar, you huff out
            of the room or try to talk to me. I've quit play-
            ing because I don't like you to feel bad. I'm fin-
            ally fed up and I want to find a way to enjoy
            playing and singing again.

Rosa: I think I do that because I feel left out. I'm tone
            deaf and I feel one-down around musical
            people.

Darlene: Oh, and I'm doubtful about my ability and I interpret your unhappiness as criticism.

Rosa: Oh, no! I think you play really well!

Darlene: I never knew that. And now that I do, I think I can play again. I *am* concerned about your feeling one-down. Is there anything I can do to make it easier for you?

Rosa: Well, I don't know right now. It already seems less of a problem now that I'm clear about feeling one-down. I can see that I'm really not. I'll think about it and let you know later if I want anything.

So what made the difference?

First, Darlene owned her anger and didn't blame Rosa. She blamed the situation.

Second, Rosa's response was non-defensive: she wasn't attacked, so she didn't feel the need to defend herself.

Third, because they both acknowledged their responsibility for their own feelings and actions, each looked within herself for the cause instead of looking within the other for the cause.

Fourth, finding the cause within herself allowed each of them to provide her own solution—hence Rosa's declining Darlene's offer for help.

The assertion that we are totally responsible for our own feelings and actions probably will sound pretty radical to some folks, so we'd like to go a little bit further in explaining why we believe it's so.

Chuck and Shirley made a date a week ago to go bowling. In the meantime, Shirley's roommate is having a small party at the apartment, and Shirley would rather be at the party without Chuck than go bowling. But she likes Chuck and wants to maintain good feelings between them. Besides, she knows she can have a good time with Chuck if she wants to.

Ten minutes before Chuck is due to arrive, he calls and says an old friend is in town for one night and he wants to spend the time with him instead. Shirley says OK, and they make a date for later. Shirley now has a smorgasbord of feelings to choose from:

> HURT, because Chuck prefers to see his old friend.
>
> ANGER that he would presume to cancel the date at the last moment.
>
> RELIEF and HAPPINESS that she can attend the party as she wanted without jeopardizing her relationship with Chuck.
>
> HAPPY that she has discovered that Chuck won't lie to her about what he wants just to "make her feel good."
>
> GUILTY that she didn't tell Chuck that she wanted to cancel the date too.
>
> ASHAMED that Chuck had the courage to do what she wouldn't do herself.
>
> ONE-DOWN, because Chuck made the move to cancel instead of her.

And probably a whole bunch more.

She will probably choose more than one of these feelings and alternate them until something else comes up to focus on. The ones she chooses will probably be the ones most familiar to her—the ones that fit her view of herself and her life. She will not be aware that she is choosing. It will appear to her that her feelings and subsequent actions are "natural," and she would be incredulous if she ever noticed that someone else responded differently.

If she feels unworthy and unlovable, she will probably concentrate on HURT and ONE-DOWN with a little ANGER now and then. Her statement to herself might be that Chuck's rejection of her proves she's unlovable, and her statement to her roommate might be, "Chuck is a son of a bitch for hurting me and disappointing me the way he did. He really makes me mad!"

If she feels worthy and lovable, she probably would have told Chuck on the phone that she was relieved, because now she could go to the party. She might say she appreciates his candor and courage and that she's looking forward to seeing him later on. She could then move into feeling happy and excited about the party.

Believing that someone else forces us to do certain things and feel certain ways is both caused by, and results in, feeling powerless and out of control in our lives.

People (all of us at one time or another) who accept this premise also believe that they can force others to behave and feel in certain ways, and the result is usually a secret agreement to struggle over who is in charge of the relationship. One person will usually take the aggressive position and one the passive position (although they can switch positions and often do).

We can get past this barrier by becoming aware of our power to decide our feelings and actions.

If I feel angry, I can also notice other feelings that I've decided not to feel and why I've elected not to feel them.

For instance, Clarice is forty minutes late and Don has been waiting. He's fuming. His inner dialog could go like this:

"I'm mad because she's late.

Why mad instead of sad or glad?

Because being late is inexcusable.

Couldn't I feel sorry for her that she would behave so badly?

Couldn't I feel sorry for me that she would treat me so badly?

When she's late, I feel like she's in charge of my life. I feel powerless, and that's scary.

Maybe I feel scared, too.

Hmmm, I can feel sorry, scared or mad and I've chosen mad. Of the three, that's the one that feels strongest to me, and when I'm feeling out of control, like I do now, I want to feel strong."

In order to do this kind of introspection, Don must:

believe that *he* decides what to feel and how to behave.

believe that *all* feelings are OK to have.

accept himself, no matter what he feels or why he feels it.

set a goal to understand his feelings and options, not to change them.

accept his mistakes as part of learning.

be willing to practice.

One more thing is extremely helpful and that is a helper— someone who is like-minded and objective and who can help him hear himself and sort out his thoughts and feelings.

If that sounds like a tall order to you, don't worry. We think it is too. It takes dedication to change life-long beliefs and patterns. Often, the kind of self-awareness that Don is using takes special training—training that's available through the various human potential theories and disciplines such as psychotherapy, counseling, sensitivity training, communications training and various self-awareness and consciousness-expanding programs.

Mistakes
are what we
make
in order
to learn.

The process of recognizing our responsibility for our feelings and actions is usually a slow one. (It is also an awakening of our innate power over our own lives.)

It is important to note that we are *not* saying that one must have fully realized one's responsibility in order to be free in one's relationships. We *are* saying that the responsibility and resulting power are *goals* to aim for, and further, that the more we recognize our responsibility, the easier it is to be free in our relationships or *anything* we do.

One more thing.

The issue of my responsibility for myself is an issue between me and me. It is utterly useless for me to remind my partner that he or she is responsible for how he or she feels or acts. It is immensely useful for me to remind *me* that *I'm* responsible for my own feelings and actions and that I'm *not* responsible for his or hers.

SECTION III

HOW TO BE
A COUPLE
&
STILL BE FREE

CHAPTER 8

PROBLEM SOLVING

Now that you've begun to know what freedom is for you, what kind of couple relationship you want, and the barriers that stop you from having both, it's time to look at a way to cross these barriers.

Section III begins with a description of techniques and procedures. Carefully followed, they can lead you past the barriers to a free couple relationship. (Although written specifically for couples, these techniques and procedures are directly applicable to problem solving with friends, children and associates—singly or in groups.)

These techniques may seem awkward or artificial to you. There are three things we want to say about that:

1. They are. Any new behavior is awkward and artificial at first, and smooths out with practice. Sometimes preplanned or structured activity is discounted as "unnatural," while old habits (beneficial or not) are thought of as "natural" simply because they flow easily and without thinking. Don't let the awkwardness put you off.

Try out these procedures. If they work for you, you can decide to stay with them until they're smooth. Keep the ones that work. Throw out the ones that don't work and look for something else. In either case, don't expect them to feel "natural" at first.

2. The procedures and techniques don't have to be followed verbatim. They don't have to be done with specific words, they have to be done with specific *intent*. For instance, if step one in the negotiating procedure is to agree to negotiate, it needn't be stated as "Do you agree to negotiate?" It can be said a lot of ways, such as, "I think we can solve this; do you want to sit down and talk it over with me?" or "What do you say we work this out?"

3. Because you are likely to be awkward at first, your friends may be awkward at your awkwardness. They may not understand. They may be impatient, scared, disoriented or something else. You may have to ask them to bear with you for a while, explain what you're doing and/or choose only your most open and forgiving friends to try things out with.

One more thing before we dive in. There is an ingredient missing from Section III—an ingredient we couldn't put there.

Your patience.

Your patience with yourself, your friend or partner, and with us.

We are asking you, our reader (and you are asking yourself) to consider a new and socially radical viewpoint—that is, (1) that there is enough to go around and that we can work together so that we can all have exactly what we want. Further, the means of doing that are mostly unfamiliar and require time and practice to make your own. And (2) that two independent people can form a lasting couple relationship without "becoming one."

That's a tall order, so please be patient.

Contract:
two or more equal parties
each giving
value in return
for value.

Open yourself and allow yourself to receive new input. Don't act at first. Let it percolate inside. Test what you're receiving in your mind. Have fantasies about using it. Finish the book. Then re-read the parts that are unclear to you.

Remember, in a counseling or class situation we would be there to encourage, support and guide you. Since we are reaching you through a book, our support, guidance and encouragement can only be general. The specifics are for you to fill in. You must be easy on yourself (selves) to be successful.

'Nuff said.

NEGOTIATING AGREEMENTS

An agreement is an understanding between two or more people about what to do and/or how to do it.

A relationship exists when people agree to do things together.

There are two important things about agreements.

One is they can be secret or they can be known. Secret ones, as we discussed, *can* cause trouble.

Two is that an agreement is a contract—two equal parties, each giving value in return for value.

We've talked about secret agreements and how to discover them. Now we'll talk about how to make overt agreements.

But first, a short digression.

If your relationship is smooth—no bumps, no lumps—don't lump it up with a "should" about negotiating overt agreements. This negotiating procedure is for use *when you have a problem* to work out with your partner. It is also an excellent mental frame of reference for establishing new, up-front relationships.

End of digression.

1. DEFINE THE PROBLEM

The first step in negotiating is for *you* to define *your* problem to *yourself*. For instance, "I want to live in a clean house and I don't want to keep it clean all by myself," or "I'm angry because she won't help me clean the house," or "I want some help keeping this house clean."

2. AGREE TO NEGOTIATE

The next step is for both people involved to agree to negotiate a solution for the specific problem. DON'T TRY TO WORK ON MORE THAN ONE PROBLEM AT A TIME. More than one gets impossibly complicated.

Usually the person with the problem approaches the other and says something like, "I have a problem about the house cleaning and I want to sit down with you and see if we can solve it together," or "I don't like the way we've established for house cleaning and I want to work out a new way. Will you help me?"

If the other person agrees, then you can proceed.

Getting agreement to negotiate is sometimes difficult at first, especially in a relationship where the partners manipulate or overpower each other to achieve their wants (and nearly all relationships have a certain amount of that).

STAGES OF
NEGOTIATION

I. Define the Problem

II. Agree to Negotiate

III. Set the Stage

    A. Time and Place
    B. Establish Good Will
    C. Reassurance
    D. Set Aside Held Anger and Hurt

IV. State (& Explore) Wants

V. Explore Options and Decide

VI. Confirm Decision and Restate

If a partner declines to negotiate, it's probably because one is afraid of being overpowered or manipulated into giving up something one wants or doing something one doesn't want. There are two things to do. One is a lot of reassurance, such as, "Look, I want you *and* me to get what we want and I think we can figure out how to do that if we sit down and think about it. How about giving it a try?" (More about reassurance in Step 3.) The other is perseverance.

When two people have interacted in a set way for some time, such as dominant and submissive, or "I'll take care of you this way and you take care of me that way," and one partner decides on a change, it may be difficult to get the other partner to even discuss it. In this case, the one wanting the change will need to be particularly objective, clear, consistent, nurturing, reassuring and PERSISTENT.

Dolores: I want to go to the Aspen Music festival for my vacation this year.

Don: I'm not interested in music.

Dolores: I'd like you to be with me, but if you'd rather go somewhere else, we can have separate vacations.

Don: Don't be silly. There are music festivals near here you can go to.

Dolores: Don, there are people performing at Aspen that I may never get a chance to hear again. I definitely want to attend that festival and I know that my vacation plans will affect you and your plans, so I want to talk it out until we are both satisfied.

Don: Well, I won't be satisfied vacationing at a music

festival, and besides, it's too far to go and too expensive.

Dolores: You don't seem to understand that it's important to me to attend that festival, and I know we can figure out how to do it without either of us sacrificing what we want. I care a lot about you and I want to do this cooperatively.

Don: Wow, I'm almost believing you're serious.

Dolores: I am serious. I want to sit down and plan this out so we are both happy about it and I want to know if you'll do that with me.

Don: Well, let me think it over.

           LATER

Dolores: Well, did you think it over?

Don: Yes, and it's out of the question.

Dolores: This vacation thing is something I've never done before, so I can see how you might misunderstand me. Don, I want you to hear me. I'm not asking for your permission, I've already decided to go. What I'm doing is offering you a chance to work out a solution that we can both be happy with. I love you, and your happiness is very important to me.

Don: Oh, well, since you put it that way . . . I guess I'll just get used to having a separate vacation this year.

Dolores: Only if you want it that way. There are other options, and I'd be happy to work with you to come up with some.

Don: Well, OK. I guess there's nothing to lose.

3. SET THE STAGE

Setting the stage is creating a safe place to talk. In a negotiation people are worried: "Will I be cheated? Will my
partner be angry if it doesn't go well? Am I 'bad' because
we haven't agreed on this? Will I be able to get what I
want?"

As long as either or both of you are afraid, the problem
solving won't go anywhere, because you won't be clear and
open about your wants. Also, it is harder to listen to your
partner's wants when you're afraid you'll be overpowered.
The suggestions that follow will help calm these fears, and
create a safe place where both of you can speak freely and
be heard.

Setting the stage is a formal process at the beginning. Later
on, you may want to be more casual. Or, with some people
it becomes a cherished ritual, and you may want to keep it
formal. However you decide to do it, remember that it is
an important step. Because the problem solving won't go
anywhere until both of you feel safe, it is also useful later in
the process, whenever you reach a place where you're both
"stuck" and don't know what else to do (an impasse). If
you stop, go back and set the stage again, you'll find the
impasse is now much easier to get through.

Setting the stage involves four things: (A) setting aside an
uninterrupted time and place, (B) establishing the good
will that exists between the partners, (C) reassuring one
another in certain specific ways, and (D) setting aside held
anger and resentment.

(A) Set aside a time and place when the negotiations won't
be interrupted. If the problem seems like a difficult one,
care should be taken that the participants aren't tired or
hassled. Just before bedtime would not be a good time, or

just before a meal when people are hungry, or right after work. Set a time when there won't be a deadline, like early evening or Saturday afternoon.

These precautions are mainly for beginners or for working out basic issues where there are strong feelings connected with the problem. After using these procedures for awhile, after you are confident that they work, negotiating can usually be done very quickly and informally.

(B) Establish the good will that exists between the participants.

If I know that you like and respect me, I will be more open to you. I will be less likely to take a defensive posture.

Likewise, if I'm feeling my good feelings toward you, I will genuinely be interested in your getting what you want.

Even if I'm angry with you about something, I can also be aware of the things about you that I like. If I cannot locate my good feelings, it is not the right time to negotiate. Either I need to resolve my conflict, or we need to call in an impartial (preferably professional) mediator.

One way to help me focus on my good will and at the same time communicate it to you is to say, "I appreciate you because _____," as many times as I can think of something to put in the blank. Remember, the purpose of this is to regenerate my good will. If I'm angry, or scared of being taken advantage of, I could sabotage this exercise. For instance, "I appreciate you because you took the trash out this week *for a change*," or "I appreciate you because you conceal your faults so well." One test of these good will statements is for the person who *receives* the statement to check it out and see how it feels. If the appreciation feels bad, then some resentment is creeping in.

I want you
and me
to both get
what we want.

This exercise won't work if my goal is to make a show of cooperating while holding on to my anger or scare. If my goal is to generate my good feelings and communicate them to you, it will work every time.

(C) It is usually necessary to reassure one another—not only at the beginning of the negotiation, but whenever an impasse occurs.

Reassurance can be anything needed that will lessen the scare, such as, "I love you"; "You are, without a doubt, the person I want for a partner"; "Just because I'm mad as hell doesn't mean I don't love you"; a hug, a wink or a present.

Often I need to tell my partner what I need for reassurance, and what I need can vary from situation to situation.

There are two specific reassurances that seem to come up a lot in negotiating.

(1) The statement, "I want you AND me to both get what we want."

(2) "I won't go away until we've made some kind of resolution." That doesn't mean I'll stay there hassling forever. It does mean that no matter how mad or hurt I feel, I won't walk out (mentally or physically) until we both feel finished, or we decide to take a break, or we give up. It is also important not to abuse this promise (e.g., making someone who must get up early stay up until the wee hours because "you promised not to go away" could make them want to avoid negotiating at all costs).

(D) Set aside held hurts and anger.

I can't negotiate about taking out the trash if I'm angry with you about the way you have or haven't been doing it.

The anger is real and cannot be denied successfully. It can, however, be dealt with (expressed) separately from the negotiating procedure. For most of us, dealing with our anger constructively is difficult and has to be learned.

A DIGRESSION ON ANGER

What to do with anger is a problem in our culture because we equate it with violence—after all, anger is usually expressed as a physical or verbal attack. Because of this, we are taught to fear our anger and keep it suppressed (unless it's thoroughly "justified"). Then, when our store of suppressed anger gets large enough, we can't hold it in any longer and it explodes all at once, thus perpetuating the belief that anger is dangerous (or at least socially unacceptable).

Although attacking is one way to express anger, the attack is not the anger. Anger is an emotion accompanied by a state of high energy—the body mobilizes itself with adrenalin and prepares to act. Anger is a response to a threat, real or imagined. The threat could be to my feeling of self worth if I feel "rejected." The threat could be that I might not, or did not, get my share of something. The threat could be to my physical well-being. Or the threat could be a possible change in a situation which I find comfortable. (Incidentally, the more competent I feel, the less often I feel threatened; therefore, the less often I feel angry.)

That's anger in a nutshell.

Now there are several things to do with anger. Briefly, they are:

HOLD IT IN. I can hold it in and let it churn inside, creating body symptoms like skin rash, respiratory problems, digestive problems, headaches, circulation problems, etc.

STORE IT UP. I can store it up until I can justify expressing it, as in "That's the last straw, I've had it!"

PHYSICALLY ATTACK SOMETHING. I can express
anger as a physical attack on something, like throwing a
book against the wall or beating up a pillow.

PHYSICALLY ATTACK MYSELF. I can express it as a
physical attack on myself, like hitting a brick wall with
my fist or going on a three-day drunk and losing my job.

PHYSICALLY ATTACK SOMEONE ELSE. I can
express it as a physical attack on someone else, like a
punch in the mouth or throwing spaghetti. A pillow
fight is sometimes helpful in letting people express their
anger toward each other harmlessly.

VERBALLY ATTACK. I can express my anger as a
verbal attack on someone else, myself or an object, such
as name-calling or threatening violence: "You're an ass
for doing that!" "I'm such a shmuck!" or "#*!! spark-
plug!"

STATEMENT OF FACT. I can express it as a statement
of fact about my feelings without aiming it at anyone or
anything, as in, "I am enraged!" "I am so goddam mad, I
could kill!" "I am really irritated because you went off
and left me!" or "I feel very angry when you leave the
bathroom in a mess!"

POSTPONE IT. I can postpone expressing it until it seems
more appropriate, such as, "I'm mad at the boss and
want to tell her without damaging my position, so I'll let
off steam privately, then work out (perhaps with a
friend) how to deal with the situation before I confront
her."

The first six choices—Hold it in, Store it up, Physically
attack something, myself or someone else and Verbally
attack—tend to create or perpetuate conflict, either
external or internal.

There are some exceptions. A physical or verbal attack can be constructive when a couple agrees to have a pillow fight or a name-calling match to let off steam so they can get on with problem solving. This is only useful when both people agree to do it for a stated purpose—often with a referee. Likewise, attacking something can be useful when a person beats up a pillow or punching bag in order to let off steam harmlessly.

Statement of fact tends to invite conflict resolution because anger is expressed without attacking. The one who is angry is taking responsibility for the anger and not making someone else responsible. It is not as difficult to hear what the problem is when the anger is expressed that way as it is when it's expressed as an attack.

Postponing tends to invite conflict resolution because it facilitates clear thinking. It's hard to think clearly in the midst of my anger. But if I go away and express my anger harmlessly, I can calm down and sort out the problem and present my case clearly.

THE MAJOR BENEFIT OF ANGER IS ACTION.

When we are angry, our bodies are stimulated and energized, ready for action. Anger leads to results. Anger can motivate change. When we are angry we want to *do something* (sadness, in contrast, produces an urge to be still, or retreat or to give up).

So look upon your anger as an asset. It can provide the necessary motivation to make desirable changes. It can motivate you to leave a relationship *or* to change the way you relate.

For more on anger, how to use it positively and express it harmlessly, you might want to read *Aggression Lab* by George Bach.

*The major benefit
of anger
is
action.*

END OF DIGRESSION.

It may be necessary to call a halt to the negotiating procedure in order to take care of built-up hurt or anger and that's OK.

Another option is to decide to set aside the hurt and/or anger and problem-solve as if the problem had no prior history—as if it's the first time it's ever come up. This may be easier to do than you think. The key is to *decide* to do it. You may slip up as you go along. If so, you can just set it aside again and go on.

4. STATE YOUR WANTS

Once the stage is set, the negotiating begins with each partner stating each one's wants about the specific problem being negotiated.

Wants are not demands.

My wanting doesn't *require* you to do anything. It is not your responsibility to see that I get what I want. At the same time, we have agreed to help each other get what we want (without sacrificing our own wants). So, if you want to have a vacation in the mountains and I want a vacation at the beach, now is the time to say so.

This is the point at which we simply state our wants; the work at this stage is refining or clarifying those wants. (Finding solutions is the step after this one.)

Barbara: "I want to vacation with you at the beach."

Mark: "I want to vacation with you in the mountains."

What looks like an impossible conflict often disappears when wants are refined and clarified. Barbara and Mark need to look for the wants *underneath* their wants. Mark can ask Barbara, or she can ask herself, "What will I get out of being at the beach?"

A likely answer would be, "I can lie in the sun, be warm and swim for exercise."

Likewise, Barbara can ask Mark, or he can ask himself, "What will I get out of being in the mountains?"

And a likely answer would be, "I can be in a peaceful place with the smell of pine trees and the sound of the breeze blowing through the trees and I can hike with you and by myself."

Now, their wants are not incompatible. For instance, a lake in a forest might satisfy both of them.

Now let's complicate the problem with this example:

Barbara: "I want a two-week vacation with just you in a quiet place at the beach."

Mark: "I want a vacation with you, but I'm not sure I want to be in total contact with you the whole time, and I've also been thinking of the mountains."

Both Barbara and Mark have refining to do. Barbara needs to look for wants underneath her want. Her want sounds like a solution to a more basic want. Mark can ask Barbara, or she can ask herself, "What will you get out of a two-week vacation with just Mark and you in a quiet place at the beach?"

A likely answer would be, (1) "I'll get two weeks of rest and peaceful relaxation with no pressure. (2) I'll have intimate contact with my favorite man any time I want it (I've missed that in the last few months because we've both been so busy). And (3) as for the beach—what I want is a warm place with plenty of sun, where I can swim for exercise and not be crowded."

Of the three wants, (1) and (3) seem to be easy to satisfy—they don't require Mark's participation. If Mark and Barbara can't agree, it is probably about (2), and the key issue there is probably "any time I want it" and "I've missed that in the last few months because we've both been so busy."

Once again Barbara needs to look for the want beneath the want and ask herself, "What will I have when I have 'intimate contact' with Mark any time I want? First, exactly what is 'intimate contact' to me?" A likely answer would be, "Intimate contact is cuddling and being cuddled, hearing and being heard, making love, being respected by someone I respect. Now, what have I got when I get all that from Mark any time I want?" And a likely answer is, "I'd have all the intimate contact I want and feel satisfied."

At this point it is possible that Barbara might realize that she wants to have two weeks of intense intimacy to make up for months of not having enough, and that her vacation want is a signal that she isn't getting what she wants in her day-to-day life.

Barbara's basic want is for loving, intimate contact in her life, and although a two-week vacation with Mark will relieve some of the pressure, it won't solve the basic problem. And the added pressure may ruin the vacation—without solving anything.

Another basic issue for Barbara: will she only allow and credit the intimate contact she has with Mark, or will she also allow and credit the intimate contact she has with her other friends? This is an important issue, because if Mark is her only resource, then she is putting Mark in charge of whether or not she gets satisfied. She will feel helpless and he will probably feel pressured. If she broadens her resources, then *she* is in charge because she has more choices and is not dependent on Mark, and Mark will find it easier to give when he is not pressured.

Now let's see what's going on with Mark. Mark has two wants, "I want a vacation with Barbara," and "I want to go to the mountains." He also has a "don't want," "I don't want total contact with Barbara the whole time."

His first want seems to be harmonious with Barbara's and probably need not be looked at any more, except as a source of reassurance. His second want, about the mountains, has to be explored because it's not compatible with Barbara's. "What will I have when I'm vacationing in the mountains? I'll have the smell of pine trees and the peaceful sound of the breeze blowing through the trees, and I can take hikes with Barbara and alone. I guess the mountains are a very peaceful place to me, and that's what I want—peace and quiet for two weeks." That seems like a basic want. It might be possible to look deeper if necessary, but in this case it probably won't be.

So, let's look at Mark's "don't want." He can ask himself, or Barbara can ask him, "If you don't want total contact, what DO you want?" "I want to be very together and intimate with Barbara sometimes and 'just around' at other times. I'd like to socialize with other people some and I want some alone time, too. I want to do a little hiking by myself. I also want to know that it's OK with Barbara if I take my own space part of the time. I'm afraid she needs me so much that she'll feel bad about it if I do. You know, sometimes I stay away from Barbara just because I feel smothered and hopeless about furnishing her the contact she needs. And then I don't get all the intimate contact with Barbara that *I* want!" (This is an example of how

*W*ants
are not
demands.

added pressure from unsolved problems could ruin the vacation.)

Let's look at Mark and Barbara's wants now and see where the conflict, if any, lies.

BARBARA
1. I want a two-week vacation with Mark.
2. I want lots of intimate contact with Mark and Mark alone.

3. I want a warm, uncrowded place where I can swim and sunbathe.

MARK
1. I want a two-week vacation with Barbara.
2. I want some intimate contact with Barbara. I want "social time" with other people, and I want "alone time."
3. I want to enjoy the pines and the mountain atmosphere and I want to hike.

The conflict seems to be with number 2 and involves a basic issue between Barbara and Mark—i.e., Barbara limits her intimate contact to Mark. Mark, feeling pressure to furnish all of Barbara's needs, withdraws and doesn't get as much contact with Barbara as *he* wants. Meanwhile, Barbara isn't getting as much intimate contact as she needs from Mark or anyone else.

Although clarification of wants and looking at options will solve this problem, it may be deep-seated and pervasive; they may need to get outside help, especially if they have a lot of stored-up anger and/or fear connected with the problem. We'll come back to Mark and Barbara later.

A WORD ABOUT VERBALIZING WANTS.

Saying our wants is usually awkward at first. We have prohibitions against it inside our heads, and overcoming those internal barriers takes a lot of energy. As a result, our statement often comes bursting out with so much energy that it sounds like an angry demand.

Here's an example:

I'm with some friends at my house and it's 10:20 p.m. I've become very sleepy. My internal rules are that a good host is congenial until the last guest leaves. If I'm sleepy, I should have another cup of coffee and not be a sissy, not indulge myself; telling my friends to go home or leaving them and going to bed is rude.

What I want is to go to bed, and I don't mind if they want to stay and have fun. I've recently learned that it's OK to get what I want and that we can probably work out a solution that satisfies everyone. I decide to overrule my internal rules and go for what I want. I have already generated a lot of energy with my internal argument, and now I up the voltage to overrule myself and say what I want. What comes out is "I'm very sleepy and can hardly stay awake. I want to go to bed," said with an intensity that implies anger to my friends. They are likely to apologize for staying so late and leave immediately.

Even if the words were softer, "I'm feeling sleepy and I wonder if you folks would mind if I went to bed and left you here to enjoy yourselves," the intensity would tend to belie my mild words, and I could get a similar reaction from my friends.

In negotiating with your partner, this "overcharge" can lead to a defensive reaction so that negotiating becomes impossible.

One way out of this dilemma is to state your wants softly and follow up (or introduce them) with a statement warning that the wants may sound like a demand but really aren't. Reaffirm your willingness to negotiate, so that you all get what you want.

An example: "Listen, gang, I have a thing about being a host which says I'm responsible for everyone's good time. So I'm afraid I won't say this right. Help me out, will you, if it sounds bad? Great. What's going on is, I'm sleepy, I want to go to bed, but I don't want to break up this party. So please feel free to stay and help yourselves and enjoy. I'm gonna go to bed. Would the last person out please turn off the lights? Thanks. Have fun."

Another way out of this dilemma is to work from your unedited list. In Chapter 4, Section II, page 46, Sara made a want list about housekeeping. Wants #3 and #7 on her list were illogical, silly, and at the same time a very clear statement of exactly what she wanted. Most *unedited* want lists will have some impossible but wonderful wants like Sara's. These wants are a key to easy negotiating.

If you and I are in the middle of a sticky problem, and I say, "I wish a wizard would show up and solve the whole thing with a wave of his magic wand, so we can get back to having fun," you will probably agree with me. This establishes step 3—setting the stage. We know instantly that we both want the same thing—a solution to our problem that will leave both of us feeling good.

The whole negotiation process then gets easier. The atmosphere feels lighter and we feel like friends teamed up to solve a problem, not antagonists.

Barbara (you remember Mark and Barbara) could say, "What we need is an ocean with a mountain in the middle of it!" or "We could rent motels at Malibu and Pike's Peak and commute by helicopter."

We all tend to take problems very seriously. Try "lightening up" and putting some laughter in the process. The more fun you have while actually negotiating, the smaller your problems will seem. Get out the munchies, put on a favorite (unobtrusive) record, relax and enjoy. Problem solving does not have to be a hassle. It's another part of loving. And loving is fun.

5. EXPLORE OPTIONS AND DECIDE.

Sometimes "the solution" pops out once the wants are clear, as in the case of Barbara and Mark and where to go for their vacation. One wants to swim at a beach and the other wants to hike in the mountains. One obvious option is to go to a lake in the mountains. *If* that satisfies them both, then the work is done.

Sometimes, options that satisfy all wants are not so obvious. When that occurs, brainstorming is an effective way to find a solution.

Brainstorming is thinking up options and writing them down. The main rule is that options that are mentioned aren't to be criticized or discussed. The idea is to come up with as many ideas as possible, no matter how impractical they may seem. What happens in this process is that the limitations we usually place on these solutions are eliminated, and ideas that we normally would have censored as being impractical are brought out and looked at.

Brainstorming is usually done with a time limit—ten minutes is good. At the end of ten minutes, if no more ideas are coming, or if there seem to be enough, the brainstorming stops and the various options are discussed. Sometimes one or two stand out as good solutions, and sometimes it's necessary to use an elimination process. Take one at a time and evaluate it until one is clearly the best solution.

As an example, let's say that Jane wants to go surfing and Fred wants to see the exhibit at the art museum.

The brainstorming might yield a list like this:

> They go to a surfing museum.
> Jane goes surfing and Fred goes to the museum separately or with a friend.
> They go surfing together today and to the museum tomorrow (or next week).
> They go to the museum early and surfing later.
> Fred goes to the museum alone (or with a friend) this morning, and they go surfing together this afternoon.
> Jane goes surfing alone (or with a friend), and Fred meets her there after he goes to the museum alone (or with a friend).

One of these options will probably satisfy them. If not, then it would be a good idea to look at the wants again and see if another want should be added, like, "I want to spend the day with you." If that is the case, then they can go back to the "wants" stage and negotiate the new wants.

Let's say that Fred is more interested in being with Jane today, and Jane is more interested in surfing (although she wants to be with Fred too). In that case, another option would be for Jane and Fred to go surfing, and for Fred (with or without Jane) to see the museum exhibit later on.

6. CONFIRM THE DECISION.

Confirming the decision involves two steps:

One, restate the decision so that both partners agree that it is, indeed, the decision: "OK, we go surfing together today, and you see the museum exhibit during the week sometime. Is that it?" "Yeah, that's it."

Two, ask yourself if the decision feels good. Is there a feeling of completion, satisfaction and/or relief about the decision? If so, you've succeeded and you can congratulate yourself and your partner. If not—if you feel tight, taken advantage of, angry, sad, scared or even vaguely uncomfortable—it may be that the decision isn't satisfactory to you. Or it could be that you think your partner "gave in" and didn't get what he or she wanted.

If the decision is a big one, allow a cooling-off period of a day or two before deciding to renegotiate. Sometimes just the long process of solving a big problem can leave you feeling uncomfortable. Make sure your discomfort is about the new solution before reopening the negotiations.

LEAVE PLENTY OF ROOM FOR MISTAKES, RE-THINKING AND REVISING IN THIS PROCESS— EVEN THE "OLD PROS" GET BOGGED DOWN FROM TIME TO TIME.

EVERYONE GETS WHAT THEY WANT

The section on Negotiating Agreements describes a procedure to follow for negotiating. This section describes a set of criteria which, when met, provide an atmosphere for negotiating in which everybody can get what they want.

These criteria were developed from Claude Steiner's "Rules for Cooperation."* To our knowledge, Steiner was the first one to say that everyone can get what they want and then explain how it can be done. We took his model and made minor changes in it to meet our needs. We present it here, with our revisions, for your use.

*Wycoff, Steiner et al., *Love, Therapy and Politics* (New York: Grove Press, 1976), pp. 28–40.

GUIDELINES FOR COOPERATION

1. Agree that there is no scarcity
2. Assume that a cooperative solution can be found
3. All solutions are renegotiable at any time
4. Equal rights and responsibility
5. Say 100% of what we want
6. No power plays
7. No rescues
8. Be willing to listen

First, a summary:

1. Agree that there is no scarcity of what we need to feel satisfied.
2. Assume that a cooperative solution can be found. If we don't know what it is, we simply need more information. (Cooperative solution does not mean compromising.)
3. Agree that all solutions reached are renegotiable at any time. Anyone who becomes dissatisfied can challenge the solution and propose a new one.
4. Agree that we have equal rights to being satisfied and that we are equally involved and equally responsible in the negotiation.
5. Agree that both of us will ask for 100% of what we want.
6. Agree that power plays (coercion and manipulation) are not an option under any circumstances.
7. Agree that there will be no rescues (no giving what hasn't been asked for and agreed to out front or agreeing when we don't want to).
8. Agree to listen and credit what each other says. It is easy to discount (out of my awareness, even) someone whose wants are scary to me.

Now a more detailed discussion of each item:

1. AGREE THAT THERE IS NO SCARCITY OF WHAT WE NEED TO FEEL SATISFIED.

Enough food.
Enough loving contact.
Enough privacy.
Enough money.
Enough of whatever we want.

This agreement is crucial to the process.

If there isn't enough, then one or both partners will get less than what they want, and the whole process is useless.

There may be times when there *is* a scarcity—there simply isn't enough to go around. At those times a cooperative solution, where everyone gets what they want, cannot be reached.

Those times are rare.

Usually the case is that there is an *apparent* scarcity—but after exploring wants and options, the scarcity disappears, or turns out to be an indicator of an underlying problem. Back in the early part of this chapter, when Mark wanted to go to the mountains and Barbara wanted to go to the beach, there was an apparent scarcity which disappeared when they discovered their basic wants and were both satisfied to go to a lake in the forest.

Their apparent scarcity about intimate contact was the result of an underlying problem in how they went about *getting* their intimate contact. They both wanted it and were going about it in a manner that left them both dissatisfied. There was no scarcity of intimate, loving contact. There was a problem in distributing it so that they both got their share.

A solvable problem at that.

Solvable *only* if both Barbara and Mark believe that it is solvable and so continue to look for a solution.

Which brings us to criteria number 2.

2. ASSUME THAT A COOPERATIVE SOLUTION CAN BE FOUND.

This is an attitude. A belief. An article of faith. A self-

*S*carcity
indicates a problem
in distribution.

fulfilling prophecy. And a reassurance when the going gets tough.

When we're at an impasse, and the negotiation is bogged down, often a restatement of our assumption will renew us: "I don't know what to do about this yet, but I do know there is a solution if we keep looking."

3. ALL SOLUTIONS ARE RENEGOTIABLE AT ANY TIME.

The negotiation can get bogged down if the partners think that the resulting decision will be forever. That would mean that they would have to cover all eventualities in that one session.

However, if we agree that all solutions are renegotiable at any time, we are free to try out solutions to see if they work and then change them if they don't. We can agree on a solution even when one of us has doubts about it working.

The "renegotiable" agreement takes a lot of pressure off the negotiation and speeds up the process.

4. AGREE THAT WE HAVE EQUAL RIGHTS TO BEING SATISFIED AND THAT WE ARE EQUALLY INVOLVED AND EQUALLY RESPONSIBLE IN THE NEGOTIATION.

This one has two parts. The first is that we have equal rights. That means that we are two equal people. We are *different* people *and* we have equal rights. That goes for all negotiators—men, women, children, bosses, employees, etc. If we are to find a solution that satisfies both of us, we must participate as equals.

The second part has to do with our commitment to work together. Cooperative problem solving requires equal energy from both partners. That doesn't mean we don't help each other over the rough places. It does mean that if I seem to be doing most of the work and/or taking most of the responsibility, I'd better stop and check with you to see what's going on so that *we* can find a remedy.

5. SAY 100% OF WHAT WE WANT.

We've talked about the importance of stating wants in negotiating. We've also talked about how and why it is often difficult to do.

We mention it here because many of us tend to understate our wants. We either aren't fully aware of our wants, feel we don't deserve to have what we want, or think we have to be "generous" and concede our share or part of our share to someone else.

At the other extreme, if I'm afraid I won't get what I want, I could overstate my want, because then if I have to compromise, I'll still get what I want.

Let's take a look at how this works.

There are six cookies. Paul wants three and Rena wants six. If Paul says he wants six in order to cover himself and Rena says she wants three because she "shouldn't" have six, then nobody knows the real wants and it's impossible to negotiate.

Paul is likely to end up with three cookies and a cup of cocoa he doesn't want and Rena with three cookies and an unfulfilled craving. In other words, neither of them got what they wanted. Paul got more than he wanted and Rena got less.

Now if both Paul and Rena had stated exactly what they wanted, they could have found options that were appropriate, like baking more cookies, making cocoa, popcorn, going to the bakery for more or a trade-off, in which the person getting the want pays for it with a back rub, etc.

Understating wants is a rescue.

Overstating wants is one kind of power play.

6. NO POWER PLAYS.

A power play is anything I do to get you to do something against your will. Our society runs (or doesn't run) on power plays, and we are all well indoctrinated in their use.

There are four types of power plays:

	OVERT	COVERT
PHYSICAL	overt physical	covert physical
MENTAL	overt mental	covert mental

An overt power play is out front and everyone knows it's taking place.

A covert power play is disguised and is often done below the awareness of everyone involved, including the perpetrator.

The physical power plays require physical action.

1. Overt physical is out front:
    a poke in the eye,
    use of weapons to threaten injury,
    a shove,
    a strike against an employer,
    a lock out,

leaving the room during a discussion,
breaking things.

2. Covert physical is physical with a secret purpose:
grabbing the check at a restaurant,
accidentally spilling something,
patting someone on the head in a patronizing way,
using body language to show another's inferiority or
helplessness, such as taking the biggest chair in the
room or standing during a discussion while someone
else is sitting.

The mental power plays are verbal or otherwise non-
physical.

3. Overt mental is out front:
"I don't like you, go away."
"If you don't do as I say, I'll tell the police what you
did."
"Charlie is such a clown, she never does anything
right."
taking a vote under majority rule (the majority powers
the minority).
Laughing at people to make them seem unimportant.

4. Covert mental is the most subtle of all:
making mistakes so that someone will do it for me,
a verbal pat on the head: "Don't worry Alphonse, I
like you,"
being frightened or angry in order to change the
subject.

Keep in mind that power plays are a response to the fear
that I won't get what I want. If I don't trust the procedure,
the person I'm negotiating with, or myself, I will probably
attempt to power play.

It is often necessary to confront a power play and follow it
up with reassurance before the problem solving can go on:

*Loving reassurance
is the
antidote.*

Bob: "I'm leaving, this is ridiculous."

Sally: "Are you leaving because you're afraid I'll take advantage of you?"

Bob: "Yes, and I'm not going to stay here and be manipulated."

At this point, it would be appropriate to look at what Bob is afraid of as well as to renew the agreement to negotiate cooperatively. It could be that out of her awareness Sally was using a covert mental power play, and Bob detected it out of his awareness and got scared. His overt physical power play might have been a response to that scare.

Since tracking down power plays tends to become blaming, it is usually far more productive to simply back off and reassure each other of our determination to *both* get what we want. That way we can side-step the power play and get on with the negotiation.

Power plays often persist.
Old habits and training die hard.
Loving reassurance is the antidote.

7. NO RESCUES.

A rescue is doing something for someone which I don't want to do. Afterward, the rescuer feels subtly cheated and/or expects to be repaid.

It is distinctly different from helping someone because I want to.

When I help someone because I want to, it's because the helping is its own reward and requires no repayment, or because we have an overt agreement about repayment.

The most common example of a rescue in negotiating is compromising—giving up some of what I want for someone else's benefit. This compromise often takes place in the rescuer's mind and is never even spoken: "I want six cookies, but there aren't enough to go around, so I'll only ask for three."

The remedy, if I'm the compromiser, is to say 100% of what I want. The remedy, if my partner is compromising, is to say that I think he isn't saying all of what he wants and to ask if that is true. He will either say yes, no or maybe, and we can proceed. Even if he denies compromising when he really is, we can proceed because it has been made clear to both of us that he is responsible for stating his wants fully and has decided to negotiate for less than he wants.

Another rescue that happens in negotiating is one person doing all the work:

Eric: "I want to eat at El Cholo."

Bob: "I don't want Mexican food."

Eric: "What *do* you want?"

Bob: "I don't know."

Eric: "Well, how about Chinese food?"

Bob: "No, I'm tired of Chinese food."

Eric: "We could get a pizza."

Bob: "Well, I don't know."

Eric is doing all the work here, while Bob is simply vetoing all suggestions.

Another example of one person doing all the work is

speaking for someone who won't speak for themself: "I know you're tired and depressed and what you need is a rest, not a hassle about who does the dishes tonight."

A remedy for this kind of rescue—if I'm the rescuer—is to say that I'm aware that I'm speaking for you (or working real hard) and you're not participating, and since I know that doing that doesn't work, I'm going to stop doing it now. Then I might ask what you want to do now. If you decline to take an active part, it might be appropriate to go back to the beginning and see if we have an agreement to negotiate, thence to setting the stage, etc.

If I'm the rescuee in this case, the remedy is to ask for a halt and state what I think is happening—that you're speaking for me and I'm not saying a word. Then search myself for what's going on with me. Am I doing a covert mental power play because I'm scared of being taken advantage of? Am I simply wanting to be taken care of right now? Would I rather be doing something else beside negotiating? Am I tired? Did I not agree to negotiate in the first place? Or what?

Perhaps my partner will help me sort this out. At any rate, once I'm resolved, we can either proceed on a new basis or reschedule the negotiation.

Rescues and power plays are a way of life for most of us.

Since they are unconscious habits, they are bound to show up in negotiating.

Learn to identify them.

Then when they come up, stop everything and start over—
    see if the problem is the same as it was,
    see if there is an agreement to negotiate,

renew the stage setting—establish good will and whatever reassurance is necessary.

Go through whatever part of the procedure is necessary to get back on the track.

8. BE WILLING TO LISTEN.

Sometimes it's hard to listen.

It's hard to hear someone say they don't like what I'm
doing (or not doing).

It's hard to hear someone say they want me to negotiate a
problem when I like the way things are and don't want to
change anything.

There are two things about listening when it's hard:

(1) We can decide to do it anyway, even if it is hard.

(2) We can make it easier by reassuring ourselves (and each
other) that we can both have what we want and that that's
what we're negotiating about.

Not listening is a sure way to discourage clear communication and to build resentments in your relationship. Check
it out. If you feel you're not hearing or being heard, SAY
IT. If you're not heard, you may have to say it loud, or
funny, or lots of times until you *are* heard. Keep saying it.
It's worth it.

PROBLEM-SOLVING DIALOGS

Now that you know the how and why of the problem-
solving procedures and requirements, you're probably
wondering what they sound like in action.

This section consists of dialogs of the process with comments interspersed to help you understand what's happening.

In order to be clear, these dialogs are condensed. Don't forget that. More often than not, (especially at first) people get tangled up or go off on a dead-end road and have to start over again.

Also, these dialogs make it look easy. That's because we chose them to demonstrate success with the process. It's important to know that in real life, in *your* life, it doesn't always flow so smoothly.

Notice that in each successful dialog at least one partner is objective and reassuring. The biggest problems happen when one or both of you don't feel willing to give. Reassurance and good will "grease the wheels." So does trust. Knowing that you're both there to find a solution makes problem solving easy. Fear that one of you wants to take advantage of the other or make the other wrong makes problem solving very rocky. All these dialogs use a lot of reassurance, love and trust to show how it's done. When you're problem solving in your own life and it's not going well, consider whether love, reassurance and trust are present. Experiment with expressing your love, reassuring yourself and your partner and expressing your trust in each other and in the process. Watch and see. The process is bound to move closer to the smooth flow demonstrated in these dialogs.

SHARON AND RALPH

SHARON: I'll be home late next Friday night, Ralph. There's an office party because Karen is leaving.

We're going out for dinner and drinks.

RALPH: What about me? What about supper? What time are you coming home?

RECOGNIZE PROBLEM

S: Ralph, that's not like you. You don't mind fixing your own supper when I go out with the girls. Is there a problem?

R: Well, I just don't like you out drinking with that bunch at the office, that's all.

S: Is that all? Can you be more specific?

STATE PROBLEM

R: (explodes) Yeah! It's that Ron—he'll be all over you, buying you drinks and laughing and joking all night.

S: Sounds like a problem, all right. Do you want to talk about it?

AGREE TO NEGOTIATE

R: You bet I do! I don't want you to go!

SET STAGE: TIME AND PLACE

S: Can we work it out now? Do you have the time?

R: Yes, let's do it.

ESTABLISH GOOD WILL
REASSURE

S: The first thing I want to say is that I love you, I'm happy here, and I'm not looking for a change.

R: (calmer) OK. Yeah. I love you, too—that's why I get so upset. You're so pretty and bright—I know other men would like to take you away from me. I don't want to lose you. Every time you go to an office party, that Ron makes a pass. I've seen him do it.

SET ASIDE HELD HURT AND ANGER

S: Ralph, I can't deal with *every* time. Can we just talk about *this* time right now? I want to find a solution that makes both of us happy. Let's start with next Friday and deal with the past events later. OK?

R: Yeah. I've been angry and worried for awhile, but I think I can put it aside. If we get this settled for Friday, it will help the whole situation.

STATE AND EXPLORE WANTS

S: OK. I want to be able to go out sometimes with the office gang— when it's necessary for my job, and also just for fun.

R: I want to feel sure that you're not cheating on me—that you won't be tempted away by one of those sharp talking salesmen. I don't want to sit home and worry about what's going on.

S: Does that mean you want to go out, too?

R: Well, maybe—I want to have fun, too.

EXPLORE OPTIONS

S: Boy, lots of ideas are occurring to me—how about these: You could come with me once in a while—maybe every third time would be OK with me. You could arrange to go out whenever I have an office party— pick a bunch of our friends and go to a ball game or a movie. Or, you could have a gang over and I'd join you when I got here. Or, you could stay home and I'd call you during the evening to let you know I care.

R: Why, Sharon, those are great ideas! You know, I love to go to the races and you don't enjoy them. If I did that, I don't think I'd feel so upset.

S: That would be fine with me, as long as you limit your losses on the bad-luck nights.

R: And maybe when I win, we could use the money for a night on the town—together.

DECIDE

S: Mmmmm—great! And later that evening I could *really* let you know I love you—a night out is just the right stimulation.

CONFIRM
DECISION

R: OK, go to your office party Friday—I'll go to the races. And if Ron comes on to you, tell him you've already got a date for Saturday night!

S: You're on, Tiger. I love you.

R: And I love you, clever woman.

MARGO AND JACK

Margo and Jack have learned to negotiate and are dealing here with a pretty basic issue between them, one which they're just beginning to explore. Their good will is readily available and they make use of it as a base for exploring and solving this one.

MARGO: I'm sleepy, how long are you going to stay up?

JACK: (nose in book) I don't know yet, I'm not sleepy and I want to read some more.

STATE PROBLEM

M: We used to go to bed at the same time and I miss that.

((Jack repeats what he thinks he heard to confirm and to let Margo know he's listening.)

J: (looking up) You miss going to bed at the same time?

STATE PROBLEM

M: Actually, I miss the snuggling before I go to sleep.

J: Yeah, that snuggling is nice isn't it? But I've noticed lately that I'm wanting more separateness from you. I feel a little panicky when we're snuggling. I can't explain it and I've been afraid to mention it 'cause you might think I don't love you anymore.

AGREE TO
NEGOTIATE

M: It's scary to hear you say that, but I guess I understand a little more about what's going on. Sounds like we've got some talking to do.

AGREE TO
NEGOTIATE

J: Yeah, and I'm a little afraid to talk about it. I'm afraid there's something wrong with what I'm feeling.

(Margo, wise lady that she is, recognizes that with both of them scared about the outcome, solving this one could take some time and their full attention. Jack agrees, and they begin setting the stage.)

M: Look, I feel good about this conversation. I think we've made a start toward solving our problem. I'm real sleepy right now, but I'd like to make a date for tomorrow right after dinner to finish this up. Is that OK with you?

SET TIME AND PLACE
REASSURE

J: Sounds great. I love you.

M: (grinning) Good night, love.

NEXT EVENING:

ESTABLISH GOOD
WILL

J: You were great last night. I had forgotten how much I appreciate your honesty and clarity. In fact, a

DEFINE PROBLEM

lot of the scare I had about talking about this is gone.

M: Me too, beautiful man. What a joy it is to be heard and then to hear you be so clear about what you're feeling.

J: I've been thinking about our conversation and about what's going on with me. I think I've been pulling away because I'm afraid of losing my independence—as if I'm taking on obligations to subordinate myself to you and our "couple-ness."

M: And when you pull away, I get scared that you don't love me or that you're angry and try to make you come back!

J: Well, I see what we're doing, and it becomes a vicious circle. But how do we get out of it?

M: Let's start with what we want. OK?

STATE WANTS

J: OK. I think what I want is reassurance from you (and myself, too, I guess) that you don't *need* me—that your happiness doesn't depend on my actions and that you love me no matter what. You know, I just realized that the more I'm certain that your love for me is unconditional, the more I want to be with you.

(*Margo paraphrases to see if she's got it and incidently helps Jack hear what he's saying.*)

M: Do you mean that you'll be reassured if I tell you that I love you and you're free to go?

J: Yes, only it's a little different. I'll be reassured if I know you love me while recognizing that you can't "let me go" because you never "had" me in the first place.

M: Look, I know I don't own you and that we are separate people. I've always been clear on that. But, we've got a deal. We're married and I'll be real disappointed if you decide to back out and that's what I'm afraid of when I feel you pulling away.

(Jack paraphrases the problem as he hears it and asks for verification.)
RESTATE PROBLEM

J: It sounds like we're each afraid of losing the other. I'm afraid I'll lose you if I separate myself from you whenever I want, and you're afraid you'll lose me if I separate myself from you. Does that sound right to you?

M: Yes.

EXPLORE OPTIONS

J: Hmm. How could I reassure you and take my space at the same time?

M: I think if you told me what you were doing—that you want some private time or some time away and that you love me and you're coming back later, I wouldn't be scared.

J: Well, that would be easy to do because it's true—I do love you and I will be back. What if I forget? Are you willing to remind me, or ask me sometimes?

DECIDE

M: Yes, I could do that, as long as I know we're sharing the responsibility and I don't have to remind you every time.

CONFIRM DECISION

J: OK, what I'll do is let you know

when I want to be separate from you and I'll remind you that I love you and that I'll be back. If I forget every once in a while, you'll remind me. Is that it?

M: Yes, we'll share the responsibility.

JEANNE AND GEORGE

Often, problems that look identical are entirely different motivationally. Compare this with Margo and Jack's discussion.

JEANNE: George, I'm going to bed now (expectant pause).

GEORGE: (engrossed in TV) uh-huh.

STATE PROBLEM

J: (Aware that she feels very bad) Uh-oh. George, I expected you to say, "OK, I'll be right there," and when you didn't, I felt awful.

G: (more attentive) Oh? is it a problem?

J: Yeah. And a scary one for me. Can we talk?

AGREE TO
NEGOTIATE
SET STAGE:
SET TIME AND PLACE

G: Sure, hon, I'll be willing to talk—but I also want to see the end of this mystery movie. It ends at 10:30. Can you wait 'til then?

J: Well, I feel pretty urgent . . . I know—If you'll reassure me a little, I think I can wait.

REASSURE

G: C'mere. (squeezes her shoulder,

hugs her) I care about you, babe. We're good at working things out. It'll be OK.

J: Whew! That's a relief. I was really scared and now I'm weepy with relief. I'm gonna go upstairs, take a special bath and pamper myself til 10:30. Maybe I'll have a good cry and see if I can get into the problem so I'll have more information.

G: OK. Take good care of yourself. I'll be up at 10:30.

LATER:

G. Here I am. That movie was a blockbuster. Do you want to talk now?

J: Yeah. I'm a lot more relaxed.

G: OK, what's going on?

STATE PROBLEM

J: Well—I'm not getting enough closeness with you lately. I keep trying to save time for us to be together, and it doesn't work. I'm afraid you don't want to be close to me anymore.

G: You know, I've noticed that you're nervous around me lately and I've felt pretty hopeless about it.

J: My memory is that we used to spend about two nights a week snuggled up together, and we'd occasionally go to bed right after supper just to be alone. I miss that. You always seem to be watching TV now.

G: Yeah. I think you're right. I've been feeling tired and disinterested. I feel lousy about it, too.

J: So what's wrong? Is it something about me?

G: No, babe, it's not. It's just the business. Money's so tight now, and all the supplies are so high priced. I'm scared that I won't be able to provide for us—and I can't get it off my mind. What kind of a partner would I be for you if I failed? I just can't think of being affectionate when I'm so worried.

J: Oh, George—I didn't know it was so bad. Have you been trying to save me from worrying? Hey, I'm a working woman myself, remember? I know it's getting tight out there. That's one reason I need our closeness. When other things are tough, I need to know we've got each other.

G: I just don't know what to do, Jeanne. I can't feel snuggly right now. I can't shake the worry.

EXPLORE OPTIONS   J: OK, What can I do to help? I love you, George, and I've got a lot to give. I can't change the economy, but maybe I can help you take the pressure off here.

G: Well, it feels better, just to know you know. I've been afraid to tell you.

J: Look, we'll be OK. No one could have been poorer than we when we first got together, and we did fine. It's not your money and success I love, hon. I'm pretty successful myself—what I need from you is caring and companionship—and if you worry yourself sick, you won't be much company for me.

G: We *did* do OK, didn't we? Actually Jeanne, I think I'll pull through this time. We may just have to cut back awhile, that's all.

J: Sure, George. We spend a lot of money that isn't necessary. Let's cut back for awhile just on general principles—for conservation's sake. More quiet dinners at home instead

DECIDE

of expensive restaurants—movies instead of night clubs. The fancy food and drink is giving me waistline trouble anyway.

G: Would you, Jeanne? You wouldn't

CONFIRM DECISION

mind? I'm suddenly remembering what a great friend and partner you've always been.

J: How would you like one of my famous foot massages? I'd love to lavish some care on you.

G: Oh great! I've always loved the way you do that. And, Jeanne, let's cancel dinner out tomorrow. I'll jog after work to relax—and then we can have the evening to ourselves.

J: You've got a date. We'll have a late dinner here, and if you'll help me cook and clean up we'll have lots of time to relax.

G: Sounds like the old days, huh? I love you, Jeanne. I guess I've missed

being real partners. I'll start sharing
my business problems with you
again.

J: Good. I guess I got into a fast-
paced life without time to share, too.
I like it better when we don't try to
protect each other. Let's face the
tough times together.

G: You've got a deal.

RAY AND JOANNA

Ray and Joanna are discovering that they don't have to do
everything as a couple and are using the negotiation procedure to help them explore this new idea. They negotiate
informally, leaving out or de-emphasizing the stages they
don't think they need.

RAY: I invited Peter to come over
Monday night to watch football.

JOANNA: You know I can't stand
being around that man.

R: Yeah, that's why I'm telling you
about it now. I thought you might
want to make other plans.

STATE PROBLEM J: I appreciate that part, but what I
don't appreciate is that I seem to
have only two choices—go somewhere else, or stay here and put up
with him.

AGREE TO NEGOTIATE R: Yeah, I see what you mean. Well,
I don't want to put you in a bind like
that, so let's figure out what to do.

J: Whew! I feel relieved to know you

want to work on this. I guess I thought it was all my problem.

STATE RAY'S PROBLEM

R: As you know, I like Peter and I haven't seen him as much since we got married—mainly because you don't like him. So what I'd like to do is figure out how I can see him more often without your being uncomfortable.

(Ray's problem is solved and Joanna's problem restated.)

J: You know, I didn't know you were missing Peter and I'm sure willing to work out something about that. In fact, I don't mind going out the night you have him over. What I mind is that you told me *after* you'd made plans.

STATE JOANNA'S PROBLEM

R: So you want to be included in the decision?

J: Right.

DECIDE

R: Well, OK. Next time I invite someone over, I'll make it subject to your input . . . and I'd like you to do the same for me.

J: OK. It's a deal. Now what about Monday night?

R: I'm negotiable, what do *you* want?

J: I want to go out. I'll check with Amy about dinner and a movie Monday night.

CONFIRM DECISION

R: OK. Peter is coming over Monday night and you're going out. If you can't find something to do, let me know. I think Peter and I could make other plans.

PEG AND TOM

Peg and Tom have a solid base of love and mutual respect. They are old hands at negotiating and do it informally.

PEG: I think you should wear a tie tonight, don't you?

TOM: Are you kidding? I haven't worn a tie for three years.

P: Yes, I know. But tonight is a special High So-sigh-ity thing.

T: So it's high society—big deal. I'm not going to dress just to be proper. You know me better than that.

(Peg senses Tom's resistance and that telling him what he should do won't work. She decides to start over and SET THE STAGE.)

P: Yes, I know that you're your own person and that you're pretty unconventional. That's one of the things I really like about you. I guess what I'm doing is asking you if you'll wear your suit and tie tonight, and I'll tell you why. Since we got the invitation, I've been thinking about when I was in high school and college and hanging out with the debutante crowd and how phony it all seemed. So, I rejected that game and every once in a while I ask myself if I pulled out because I couldn't hack it or if I really tried it and found it lacking. So, tonight I want to play the society game all the way. I want to remind myself that I can hack it if I want to.

(Peg and Tom both feel the truth and good will in this statement, and it lays the groundwork for Tom to hear Peg's wants and Peg to respect Tom's wants.)

STATE PROBLEM

STATE WANT

AGREE TO NEGOTIATE EXPLORE OPTIONS

T: OK. I hear you and I don't mind wearing a suit and tie for *you*. I wouldn't do it for *them*, though.

EXPLORE OPTIONS

Maybe I'm scared *I* can't hack it—even in a suit and tie. Looks like tonight could be an interesting experience for both of us.

P: You're fantastic! And you know, I hadn't realized exactly *why* I wanted you to dress up, but now that I do, l realize that I really don't need to remind myself in that way. I know I could make it if I wanted to. So, I guess that means that if you have second thoughts about the coat and tie, it's OK with me. My first choice is still to put on the dog, though.

DECIDE

T: Let's show 'em and ourselves, too.

VALERIE AND TAMARA

Sometimes we have a value standard or judgment that doesn't hold up in the cold, clear light of objective thinking. Some are subtle and some are not. In this example, Valerie is trying to impose an unexamined value on Tamara.

STATE PROBLEM

VALERIE: I hate it when you chew gum.

TAMARA: What?

V: I think you look crude when you chew gum.

(asks for clarification.)

T: How is that?

V: Chewing gum makes people look low class and unsophisticated.

If Valerie had said, "You open your mouth real wide and

make noticeable sounds with every chew and seem totally unaware of how you look and sound," then there would have been a different problem to discuss. However, we assume that this isn't the case, since Valerie's objection is to *anyone* chewing gum in *any* manner, as a matter of principle.

(This dialog doesn't get into the problem-solving process because the criteria aren't met—Tamara is working to get a clear statement of the problem.)

T: Says who?

V: Anyone with class.

T: I don't buy it.

V: I feel terrible when I see you fouling up your image like that.

T: I still don't buy it. I think you got some misinformation somewhere about that.

V: You don't think people who chew gum look crude?

T: I suppose that it's possible to chew gum so that it looks crude, but I don't think I do it that way.

V: Hmmm, maybe it is possible to chew gum without looking crude. I'll give it some thought.

Tamara's firmness gives Valerie a chance to question her assumption. If Tamara had been afraid that maybe Valerie was right, they could have ended in an argument about who was right and who was wrong.

FRED AND CAROL

One of the advantages of the negotiating process is that it keeps getting better and better.

Fred and Carol are experts at negotiating. They care about each other and they've been doing cooperative problem solving for several years.

In the process, they've learned to trust each other to such a degree that they can help each other with problems on a deep emotional level.

Therefore, when Carol uncovers some deep-seated emotional/sexual turmoil, her first thought is to go to Fred for help and loving support. Notice that establishing good will happens all throughout this dialog. It's a natural result of Fred and Carol's good feelings for each other.

SET THE STAGE: ASK FOR TIME AND PLACE, BEGIN TO STATE PROBLEM REQUEST GOOD WILL

AGREE TO NEGOTIATE AGREE ON TIME AND PLACE ESTABLISH GOOD WILL ESTABLISH GOOD WILL

DEFINE PROBLEM FURTHER

ESTABLISH GOOD WILL

CAROL: Fred, I want some time to talk to you about a problem I have. It's about sex, and I'm scared to mention it, so find a time when you've got the energy to be extra understanding, OK?

FRED: Sure, honey—I feel fine right now—and I have lots of energy for keeping our sex life good for both of us. Would it be easier for you if I held you while we talked?

C: Oh, lover, what a great idea. I feel so safe when you hold me. I know this issue has to do with lots of confusion I have in myself—most of it is not related to you, except that it affects my response to you sexually, and that *does* involve you.

F: It sure does, hon. Besides, I care about you and your happiness— neither of us is completely free of confusion. You always help me with mine. I'm glad to be able to love you enough to help. Come on, what is it —I can take it—especially if you're gentle, too.

**ASK FOR DEFINI-
TION OF PROBLEM**

C: Well . . . it's . . . oh, God, it's hard to expose this side of me. If you weren't so clear and loving I'd never have the courage. (takes a breath and plunges) Well, I've been reading about women's sexuality and I've come to some realizations about my self-image. I want to change and be more free. I've become aware that I feel bad about my vagina. The feelings go so deep, there aren't even any reasons. I feel dirty, smelly and ugly "down there"—the sex problem happens when we have oral sex. I can't believe you like cunnilingus and I feel guilty about enjoying it—I clench, and it's almost impossible to have an orgasm. I've even faked it, just so you'd stop.

DEFINE PROBLEM

EXPLORE WANTS

F: Oh, poor baby! I didn't realize you were having problems. I *have* been a little confused because you don't seem eager for it. How can I help?

STATE WANTS

C: I guess the first thing I need is to know how you really feel—*do* I smell bad? Do you like it, or do you just do it because I'm supposed to like it? The worst part is, I don't even know if I'll believe you—I'm so guilt-ridden and confused.

EXPLORE OPTIONS

F: Well, I have a couple of ideas. First, logic. You like giving *me* head, don't you?

C: You know I do—I do it often enough.

F: Well, think about why *you* like it. Part of it, I know, is because *I* like it so much, and you like to give me pleasure.

C: Right—but I also like other things about it—textures and sensations.

F: Right. It's the same for me. There are two aspects. The pleasure I get from giving you pleasure—and the pleasure of the act itself. I've got an

EXPLORE OPTIONS

idea about showing you that. I suggest we take a shower and go to bed. We'll use a mirror so you can see yourself, and you can ask all the questions you want. Do you think that will help?

EXPLORE OPTIONS

C: Can we stop or back up if I get scared?

CONFIRM DECISION

F: Of course, love. This session will be on your terms. You asked for reassurance and information, and I want to do this with you.

C: Ooh! I'm getting turned on, you silver-tongued fox!

F: Come with me, babe—there's something beautiful I want to show you.

PETE AND ETHEL

We are not always aware that we have a problem until we notice that we are angry, weepy, guarded around our partner, or otherwise emotional. A person with a problem can be so emotional and confused that one cannot sort out the problem from its effects. In that case, we can "get a little help from our friends."

The following two conversations only get as far as the appointment to figure out and negotiate the problem. Yet it's easy to see that these couples are well on their way to finding out what the problem is and then solving it.

PETE: Hi, hon, I'm home. What's for dinner?

STATE PROBLEM
(Confused announcement that there is a problem.)

ETHEL: Nothing! I've been crying all afternoon. I haven't fixed anything.

ASK FOR DEFINITION OF PROBLEM
(Pete shows he heard— nice reaction to a surprise event.)

P: Uh-oh. Sounds like a problem. What's wrong?

DEFINE PROBLEM
(Statement of confusion.)

E: I wish I knew. I feel miserable. I couldn't wait for you to get home, and I didn't want to see you at all— I'm all mixed up—I don't know what's wrong.

AGREE TO NEGOTIATE
(Pete doesn't jump in and rescue, he makes a caring offer.)

P: Well, would you like me to help you find out?

AGREE TO NEGOTIATE
(Ethel is clear about feeling ambivalent and takes responsibility for her confusion.)

E: I'm not sure I want to know. I'm scared. Oh, yes, of course I do want your help. And I do want to find out. I'm just mixed up and feeling helpless.

DEFINE PROBLEM
(Pete starts asking
questions which Ethel will
need to think about—it
helps her get out of emotion
and into clear thinking.)
(Ethel is now thinking
about what's happening.)

(Pete repeats what he's
heard and again asks for
thinking.)

(Another clear-thinking
evaluation by Ethel.)

(Pete realizes that neither
of them has the energy to
problem-solve, so offers a
way to get re-energized.
Explores options.)
SET TIME AND
PLACE
(Now Ethel is offering
options, too. She's not
overwhelmed by her
depression and can think
clearly. She offers an
appointment to negotiate
and work on problem.)
(Pete agrees, showing that
he feels benefitted, too.)
AGREE TO
NEGOTIATE

P: Well, let's start with the obvious. Is your health OK? Have you gotten enough sleep?

E: Not really, but I don't know which came first—feeling depressed or losing sleep—it feels like a circle.

P: OK, it sounds like an emotional hassle aggravated by lack of sleep. What do you think?

E: I guess so. I'm feeling guilty because I'm not supposed to lose sleep or feel bad. You deserve to rest after your workday, and I'm not helping.

P: Right—I'm tired, too. I suggest we call out for dinner to be delivered, and go to bed early. Does that sound good?

E: Oh, wonderful, Pete! And tomorrow's Saturday, so let's cancel our date with the Smiths and stay home. I think I need time to be with you and talk. I feel the need for some kind of change and I want your help finding out what it is.

P: Sounds great to me. I could use a relaxing Saturday, myself.

SCOTTY AND DAVID

(Scotty begins to realize that there is an underlying problem.)

(David begins to search for the problem.)

AGREE TO
NEGOTIATE

SCOTTY: (shouting from the bedroom) David, did you just turn the stereo off?

DAVID: Yeah.

S: (puzzled and irritated) I was listening to it, what's going on?

D: I hate heavy metal.

S: David! My music never bothered you before!

D: Well, it does now!

S: (calmly) David, what's different now? What's changed?

D: I'm pissed off now!

S: What about?

D: I don't know, but I've been mad at you for several days. (begins to calm down) I haven't said anything because I couldn't justify it.

S: Do you want to sort it out and see if we can solve it together?

D: Yeah, but not now. I want to cool off and figure out what I'm mad about.

S: Will you turn the music back on again?

D: Would you settle for something a little more mellow 'til I cool down?

If Scotty had been angry too, or defensive, this dialog could have gotten into a tangle of accusations and bad feelings. The tangle and bad feelings would continue until one or both of them started thinking about defining and solving the problem and/or feeling their good will for the other—not an easy thing to do sometimes, but essential if the problem is to be solved.

MYRA AND JOE

Often, having an argument is how we discover that there's a problem. It may not be the smoothest way to get to problem solving, but it certainly makes the problem impossible to ignore.

MYRA: Joe, the garbage is overflowing in the kitchen again! Will you take it out?

JOE: Yeah, yeah, in a minute. The ball game's on.

M: You never take it out when you should! I'm sick of this mess! It's always a ball game or something else! You're just lazy!

J: Leave me alone! You're always bitching about the garbage or something—can't a guy have some peace and quiet?

M: I'm mad, Joe! I'm not gonna leave you alone until you take out the garbage!

J: Take the garbage out yourself— I'm going to the bar, where I can watch the game in peace and quiet. (Joe storms out and Myra cries)

NEXT MORNING

SET THE STAGE   JOE: Myra, I'm just miserable about last night.

MYRA: Me, too. I'm mad and hurt and hopeless.

REASSURE

J: Does it help to know that I love you and want to sort out what that was all about?

M: Yeah, it does. It gives me hope.

J: Why don't we go back to the beginning and start over.

AGREE TO
NEGOTIATE

M: OK.

DEFINE PROBLEM

J: My problem was being interrupted while I was watching the game. I guess I was frustrated and pissed off about that.

DEFINE PROBLEM

M: My problem is that the garbage basket gets full and you don't take it out like you're supposed to and my kitchen looks terrible and smells bad. I got mad because it happens a lot.

J: Look, my problem about being interrupted is over with. So, let's go ahead and talk about yours, OK?

DECIDE ON
PROBLEM TO
NEGOTIATE

M: Yeah, OK.

J: I don't really like taking out the garbage, but I'm willing to do it. It's just that it always seems to sneak up on me, and when you get angry, I get stubborn.

ESTABLISH GOOD
WILL

M: Boy, do I know it. I'd sure like to find a solution that keeps us from fighting. I like spending time with you, and this messes it up.

J: Yeah. I'd rather you sat with me during the ball game and snuggled. I like being with you when everything's OK.

DEFINE PROBLEM

M: You said the garbage sneaks up on you—does that mean you don't know when it's getting full?

J: Yeah. I look at it sometimes and it's fine. Then a couple of hours later it's full and you're mad.

M: Well, I know when it fills up—when I make dinner—and when I scrape the dishes after dinner it's usually full.

EXPLORE OPTIONS

J: Oh, you mean it's that regular? Well, maybe I could take it out right after dinner every night—while you're doing the dishes.

M: That would fix it most times—but what if something unusual happens and it gets full at a different time?

DECIDE

J: Well, if I take it out every night after dinner, would you be willing to let me know when it gets full any other time, and *then* trust me to take it out without being nagged?

DECIDE

M: Well, the only time that wouldn't be good enough is when we're having company. So, on those times, I can ask you to do it right away, *and*, if you're really busy or unavailable, I wouldn't mind taking it out—as long as you did it cheerfully most of the time.

CONFIRM DECISION

J: Well, let's try that. I'll take it out every night after supper and see how it works. I'll try it for a week, and then we can see if we're both satisfied. OK?

CONFIRM DECISION   M: Great! Does that start tonight?
CONFIRM DECISION   J: Sure does—as soon as you feed me, woman, I'll take the garbage out. Then maybe we can snuggle and watch TV. OK?

ANN AND CARLA

Sometimes couples don't get as far as the agreement to negotiate. In this case, Carla is unwilling to take responsibility for her actions, and Ann is so angry, she merely aggravates the problem.

(Angry and accusing—states anger—problem sounds like Carla's because Ann hasn't recognized her own problem yet.)

ANN: I've been standing here waiting for 45 minutes. You said you'd be here at 3 and it's 3:45. I'm angry because I believe you make yourself late sometimes and leave me waiting, or make both of us late when we have to be somewhere.

(Takes blame, but does not offer to negotiate or solve problem.)

CARLA: I'm really sorry. One thing led to another and I lost track of time.

(Her anger is still blocking effective statement of her problem.)

A: Yes, you do that a lot, and sometimes when you do, you leave me hanging—or cause me to be late, and I don't like it. In fact, I'm mad as hell about it. I know you can be on time if you want to be!

(Still apologizing rather than negotiating.)

C: What can I say? You're right to be angry. But I don't do it on purpose. I just lose track of time sometimes.

A: What makes me so mad is that

you won't take responsibility for being late! If you would, we could probably work this out.

C: Well, you don't think I'm late on purpose, do you?

A: Yes I do, and if you didn't turn off your mind about it, you'd recognize it!

This discussion could go on indefinitely, unless one of them decides to switch directions. At this point Ann is angry and accusing—although she is clear about her anger —and Carla is defensive and passive. Chances are this is a familiar conversation for them.

Let's see what happens if Ann switches from accusing to problem solving.

(Breaks pattern!)
ESTABLISHES GOOD WILL

STATES PROBLEM
(Still threatening somewhat, not perfect.)

ANN: Look, Carla, I love you a lot and I want you to be sure of that. Our relationship is in trouble because of this problem. I'm not willing to put myself in situations where I'm left in the lurch and I can't figure out how to be with you without it happening sometimes. I want you to know that I'm seriously considering leaving if we can't find a solution to this problem.

(Still taking blame.)

CARLA: I didn't know you felt *that* strongly about it. I'll try to be on time from now on. I promise.

(Asks for AGREEMENT TO NEGOTIATE.)

A: No, Carla, "promising to try" is just the same old thing. What I want is to negotiate a solution that we both believe is workable. I'm not demanding that *you* change. I'm asking that you sit down with me and look for a way for both of us to be satisfied. Maybe I can do something different, too.

(Declines to negotiate—hangs on to old pattern.)

C: I don't know what you could do differently, Ann, it's probably all my fault.

REASSURES
(Tries again to open negotiation.)

A: I don't know what I could do differently either, but I know there's something. We built this problem together and we can fix it together, too. Are you willing to sit down with me and work 'til we solve this?

(Declines again.)

C: I think it's all my fault and I'm going to do better, Ann. The only solution is for me to be on time from now on.

(Ann realizes that she's not going to get an agreement to negotiate, so decides to explore options she has on her own.)

A: I can't solve this cooperatively without your help and energy, Carla, and I'm angry and frustrated, so I'm going to figure out how to solve it for *me* on my own. I'll let you know how I decide to handle it. In the meantime, if you decide we *can* solve it together and you're willing to negotiate a solution that suits both of us, let me know.

LATER:

ANN: I want you to know I've got a solution for myself about our lateness hassle. It's one-sided, and I don't think it's the best possible thing—it's just a way to protect my-

self and keep from building up anger
—do you want to hear it?

CARLA: Sure.

A: I am not going to make appointments with you unless there's an
alternative in case you're late. For
example, if you're not there by a certain time, I go by myself, and you
can arrive on your own schedule.
That keeps me from waiting around.
It also means I won't get myself into
situations where I'm dependent on
your promptness.

C: OK, Ann. But it won't ever happen again, so you won't need that
solution.

A: At this point, Carla, I'm not
ready to believe that 'til I see it—but
if you want to offer a solution of
your own, I'm renegotiable any time.

Ann has done a good job of getting out of her old habit of
impotent anger and getting into taking care of herself. She
has unhooked herself from depending on Carla to be on
time and has left the door open for Carla to change her
position and negotiate. There's a good chance that when
Carla sees that Ann doesn't get angry any more, she'll be
able to break her pattern and negotiate a solution.

RUTH AND HENRY

What happens when other people are around and a problem arises? Consider Ruth and Henry, who are at home
preparing to leave for a party. The babysitter, Jennie, is in
the room with them.

HENRY: C'mon, Ruth, we'll be late.

RUTH: (with a flourish) Here I am!

H: You can't wear *that* to the party! My God, there's nothing to it! You're nearly naked!

JENNIE: Oh, Mrs. Jones, you look wonderful! He's just jealous. Ignore him.

R: Henry, you're serious, aren't you? Are you really unhappy about the the way I look?

H: No, Ruth—I think you look wonderful! I'm just not willing to let other people see you like that!

J: Oh, Mr. Jones, don't be silly. Everyone dresses like that now.

R: Jennie, I don't want to be rude, and I appreciate your compliments. However, Mr. Jones and I need to work this out. His feelings are very important to me. Would you mind letting us discuss this ourselves?

J: Oh. Sure, I'm sorry.

R: Thank you, Jennie. Now, Henry, let's talk about this.

The cooperative problem-solving process can now begin.

MARTHA AND GARY

Sometimes the most difficult part of negotiation is getting to the agreement to negotiate. Notice how Martha keeps her cool and focuses on her goal despite Gary's attempts to avoid the topic. Also notice her clarity and conviction—

they make her statements impossible to ignore or misunderstand.

SET TIME *AND PLACE*	MARTHA: Gary, I want to talk to you. GARY: Sure, go ahead—I've always got time to listen to the little woman.
STATE PROBLEM	M: Gary, I want to get a job. G: Oh, Martha, you're not serious. What do you want, more money for new clothes?
STATE PROBLEM	M: No, Gary, I want to get a job. I want to get out of the house and meet people. I want to have a career. G: Now, now, Martha—why don't we just go out to dinner tonight? M: Gary, please listen to me. I'm serious. G: Is it your time of the month? You seem upset.
STATE PROBLEM	M: Gary, I am not having emotional, physical or mental problems. I have made a decision about my lifestyle, and that involves you. I want your cooperation. I want you to know I am firm about this and I will stay here until you agree to discuss the matter with me like two adults. G: Gee, Martha, I guess you are serious. But how can you mean it? VanDerGelder women have never worked—my mother took pride in her house and children—she didn't need to work.
STATE PROBLEM	M: Gary, your mother was a fine

woman. And so am I. These are different times. I want a new challenge. A maid can keep house, and the children are all active teenagers. They don't need me. I need to feel productive again.

G: But, Martha, what will my business associates think? What about our position? Who will take care of me?

REASSURE

M: I don't want to discomfort or embarrass you. Let's sit down and discuss it, and I'm sure we can work it out. We're both intelligent and creative. A solution that pleases both of us won't be hard to find.

AGREE TO
NEGOTIATE

G: Well, all right. I don't like it, but I'm willing to discuss it.

MARVIN AND CLAIRE

Some problems are not solvable in one sitting. Here, Claire and Marvin negotiate a frightening problem. Their emphasis is on reassurance and leaving room for lots of renegotiation.

SET TIME AND PLACE

CLAIRE: Marvin, can we talk?

MARVIN: Yeah, we need to. You've been quiet all week. What's up?

STATE PROBLEM
REASSURE
ESTABLISH GOOD
WILL

C: Hon, I've got an itch. We've been together a long time. It's great being with you, I love you. I enjoy your company. The problem is that I'm curious about other men. One man in particular. I'd like to see what sleeping with him is like.

AGREE TO NEGOTIATE *(implied)*

M: Wow—you get right to the point, don't you? Give me a minute to absorb that.

C: Yeah, I'm sorry. It was so hard to get out, it just came out all at once—forgive my clumsiness. I'm scared, Marvin—and yet I'm unwilling to ignore this any longer. I'm unhappy and restless. I don't want to hurt what we have—yet my wanderlust will do that anyway if I just ignore it.

M: Boy, you're in a tight place. I don't know whether to comfort you, get mad at you, or curl up in the corner in a fetal position. God,

EXPLORE OPTIONS

Claire, isn't there some other way to do it? Do you have to have another man? Can't you be happy with me? You always were before. Damn that job of yours! It *has* to be someone there!

STATE AND EXPLORE WANTS

C: Marvin, I'm not sure what it is. I've never felt the need before—and there have always been attractive men. This feels like something inside myself I need to satisfy. You're right. I always *was* happy. You've always been a great husband, friend and lover. I've been kicking myself for weeks—and I haven't been able to talk myself out of it. I even thought about sneaking—but I decided that was too nasty. I want to be honest.

M: Well, what now?

C: I want to try it once. I'm not going to give you details—there's no point in torturing you. I'm not doing this because of you—just because of me.

STATE WANTS

M: But I don't want to wonder about when and how, or if it was good. Clare—you could decide he's better than me. I could lose you.

C: Yeah, I'm scared about that, too. I don't think it will be that way. I love you too much to throw it away easily. Still, it's got to be considered.

EXPLORE OPTIONS
CONSIDER
RENEGOTIATION
AS AN OPTION

This is a big change for us. What I want is to sit down after my experiment and talk again. I think that at that point I'll know what I'm trying to find, and I think I'll be able to reassure both of us then.

M: Look, I love you. I want you to be happy. If you need to do this, I guess I can stand it. And I would like to talk again afterwards. I may not be able to handle this very well.

ESTABLISH GOOD
WILL
DECIDE TO
EXPERIMENT
(with reservations)
REASSURE
ESTABLISH GOOD
WILL
AGREE TO
RENEGOTIATE

C: Marvin, you are a brave and loving man. You're so precious to me. This is my problem, and I'm creating a problem that you have to face, so I have a lot of willingness to give to you. If you're upset at any time, we'll talk. I'm willing to discuss this every day, if we need to, until we both understand what's happening.

M: I want you to know this hurts. And I love you. And I know I couldn't hold you against your will. I'll be anxious until we talk again. And I'm not used to praying, but I think I will about this one.

C: I love you, Marvin, and I'm sorry my confusion is a problem for you. I want you to know I'm doing my best to resolve this and to keep our relationship solid.

CHAPTER 9

GOALS

This chapter is about feeling successful.

The essence of it is that if we have a goal, and if we stop and take notice when we achieve that goal, then we will feel successful.

A long-term goal is important. Short-term goals are perhaps even more important—*do-able, reasonable*, short-term goals. With short-term goals, we can experience our success regularly as we go along—or if we're not achieving our short-term goals, we can back off and try something different.

Many people set goals easily and naturally. Some may need to practice doing it self-consciously until they get used to the process. However, the problems with goals are not usually in setting them. The problems are usually in making them reasonable and do-able, and in noticing and rewarding ourselves when a goal is reached.

If my long range-goal is to get a college degree, my short-range goals might be (1) to finish my freshman year; and shorter, (2) to do well on my term paper in English Composition; and shorter still, (3) to make sure I know the material to be covered this week. Then it is important to notice when I achieve each goal and to congratulate myself each time. It is a temptation to do neither, to take my accomplishment for granted and immediately shift my focus to the next goal. If I follow my temptation, I may never feel successful, and only feel burdened by a never-ending set of tasks. Most of us tend to ignore our small accomplishments and stress our small failures (it's "How terrible!" for a D on a paper, and "It's about time!" when we get an A).

A common goal for couples is making a baby. Short-term goals would be conceiving the child, learning husband-coached childbirth, learning about child care and child development, taking a parenting class, finding a name, etc. Of course, each of these steps can be broken down into shorter goals if necessary or desirable.

Then if each small success is celebrated, the whole experience can be felt as rewarding and much less as "waiting for the baby to come." Also, when the baby arrives, the parents can take full credit for their own personal success in addition to celebrating the new life.

It is also useful to set goals about the "process." In the case of making a baby, the partners could set the goals of keeping the mother in good health, communicating with each other about emotional and physical changes, both partners being involved with the pregnancy as much as possible and the father helping with the birth event.

With goals such as these—even if the pregnancy isn't successful—the parents have the togetherness and shared experience of this process. They have learned from it, they can fully share their disappointment and can plan the next goals.

If the pregnancy is successful, the parents have that satisfaction to add to their closeness. They feel successful and

*Celebrate
small
victories.*

recognized by each other. The baby gets a share of the attention, but not all of it, and no one is drained.

Part (perhaps all) of the cause of "post-partum blues" is that the loving attention shifts from the mother to the baby at the moment of birth, and the mother, having done the work, goes from feast to famine in terms of loving attention at a time when she is exhausted and needs extra love.

Focusing on and celebrating success can keep this from happening.

Pregnancy is an easy, tangible example. But there are many goals which are intangible, such as personal growth, personal contentment, spiritual development, dynamic life-style, loving security base, excitement, sexual expression, maintaining a specific lifestyle, having fun, feeling independent, etc.

Intangibles become tangible when seen in terms of short-term goals. If your overall goal is personal independence within the intimate couple framework, a short-term goal might be feeling good (or comfortable) about spending evenings separate, and then sharing experiences about it. Another might be cultivating separate friends as well as couple-friends. Also, enjoying different interests and opinions while keeping communications open. For instance, if she's a Democrat and he's a Republican, and they discuss the pros and cons of each party, both become more informed as a result. They stimulate each other to think and examine their preferences.

If both are clear that individuality is their goal, then actions in that direction won't be misunderstood. In a politically minded couple, for instance, if he's a Conservative and she becomes a Liberal, they have a potential problem. He could see her choice as defiance, anger or putting his ideas down. If, however, they have agreed to develop their individuality, her choice becomes part of their goal, and they can both be interested and amused by party comparisons.

CHAPTER 10

COMMITMENT

First, let's clarify what *commitment* means.

Literally, it means a pledge, promise or statement of intent.

In a traditional relationship, it usually implies the marriage vow or something relative to permanence and exclusiveness:

> "I do take thee for my lawful wedded wife/husband,
> for better or worse,
> for richer or poorer,
> in sickness and health,
> till death do us part."

It is this vague, all-inclusive, permanent obligation that the word *commitment* implies which makes it difficult to use in discussing freedom in a couple relationship.

We can only use the word when we recognize that although it means a pledge, promise or statement of intent, it *doesn't* imply what the commitment is to.

So, in a free relationship, each couple will have a different set of agreements to which they've committed themselves. One couple will agree to their own form of monogamy.

Another couple will agree to help each other in certain ways for a certain period. Another will agree to raise a family together for as long as that takes. Still another will agree to a one-day-at-a-time relationship. And each of these couples will have their own sub-agreements which are harmonious with their basic agreement(s).

When people ask about commitment in a "free couple" relationship, they are usually talking about permanence: "Will you stick with me when the going gets tough, or will you go away and try to find someone who's easier to get along with?" "If we're not getting along, how long will I stay to work it out before I get up and leave?" "What if I find out I can't get what I want with you?" and "What if Prince (or Princess) Charming comes along?"

We (Tina and Riley) have no pat answer for these kinds of questions. We don't know how to solve hypothetical future problems.

Our conclusion is that one of the characteristics of coupling and freedom is that there are no guarantees about the future short of what we both specifically agree upon—such as raising children until the youngest reaches 18, or taking care of each other in our old age. And, of course, all agreements are renegotiable at any time—renegotiable to the satisfaction of all parties.

For free couples who agree that they want their partnership to last until one of them dies, and that they'll hang in there no matter what, the longevity problem has been solved (unless one or both change their minds).

If they both change their minds, there's no problem.

But if one partner changes one's mind and the other wants to keep the same agreement, there is a problem to negotiate.

Let's assume that John and Mary have a free couple partnership, so that John's problem is not a surprise to either
of them.

John: I've been thinking that it's time for me to move
        on. We've been wrestling with this problem of no
        sex life for months, and I feel hopeless about get-
        ting what I want with you.
Mary: Oh, I don't want you to go. And I understand
        your hopelessness. I've been feeling dissatisfied
        and hopeless too.
John: After all our efforts to change, do you still believe
        that we can both get what we want?
Mary: If only you'd be more tender and patient!
John: If only you'd be more responsive and assertive!
        Mary, we've been over this time and time again,
        and I feel hopeless now.
Mary: There are so many good things about our partner-
        ship. I'm afraid I'll never have them with anyone
        else. Those good things outweigh our sex problem
        for me.
John: You'd compromise and settle for less than you
        want because you're scared you couldn't find
        someone else?
Mary: Yes, I would.
John: I've thought it over a lot lately and I'm just not
        willing to compromise. Do you understand, Mary?
Mary: (with tears) Yes, I understand. One of the things I
        love about you is your unwillingness to compro-
        mise. You've helped me learn to go for what I
        want.
John: (with tears) Yes, and you're good at it. You never
        have to compromise any more. You could find the
        kind of tender, patient man you want. I'm sorry
        I'm not the way you want me to be, but I just can't

be someone I'm not and I feel terrible knowing
you feel pressured to act different than you feel.

Mary: (crying) Oh, John, I don't want you to go.

John: If I could think of another way to get what I want,
I'd stay. But I feel utterly hopeless. Do you think
there's any possibility that we could both get what
we want?

Mary: Not really, John.

As in all negotiations, there are several ways this situation
could go. Mary and John could agree to a last big effort
and go to a sex clinic. They could agree to the parting and
feel like failures. Mary could feel rejected and fight the
parting, while John sadly (and perhaps with guilt) makes a
unilateral decision in his own behalf. Those roles could be
reversed. Or, they could agree to the parting, grieving
their loss, but feeling powerful about taking positive action in their own behalf and successful about the goals
they did achieve together.

To sum up our position on "permanent" relationships:

We believe that all relationships change, if not by unilateral or bilateral decision of the partners, then eventually
by the death of one (or both).

We believe that there are no guarantees in life. Everything
will change sooner or later, although we often pretend that
it won't. We believe that people imagine permanence in
order to feel more in control of the world. We are often
afraid when we think that our comfortable position might
change, so we try to make it permanent—alas.

We believe (if you recall the bias section) that the health
and growth of an individual is more important than the
well-being of a couple, and that a relationship that restricts
that health and growth must change in some positive way
so that both of its members benefit.

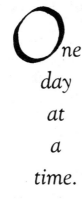

O*ne*
day
at
a
time.
(stolen from Alcoholics Anonymous)

Based on these beliefs, we offer in this book a technique for successful relationships one day, one solution, one success at a time.

We offer this in hope that at the end of your life, you can look back over a succession of problems solved and victories achieved that lead from where you are now to where you will be then.

You see, we don't advocate long-term relationships per se. What we advocate is long-term lives filled with satisfaction and success.

CHAPTER 11

LOVE

Love is.
Really.
Love simply is.
Everywhere.
Everyone is lovable (some of us believe we are not and act as if we are not, thereby concealing our lovableness). Everyone is loving (some of us hide our loving nature behind anger, fear or numbness, and some of us just don't know how).

When we accept that love is, it's just a matter of time and effort before we find it in ourselves and each other.
This acceptance we call trust.
Without love, that is, without trust, there can be no freedom in coupling, intimacy or commitment.

Because once I trust, I no longer need to be other than I am. I know that you accept me the way I am.

Even if you seem to object to me—are angry at me or disgusted or distant—I know that you feel loving to me underneath, and that we simply need to find out what the problem is and solve it.

So, at the core of coupling as free people is love.

It is the fuel of a free couple relationship.
Without it, freedom cannot be.
And the extent to which love (and trust) is known to and enjoyed by a couple is the extent to which the partners are free.

Loving and being loved may be a problem for you. It is for most of us. Usually, when we don't experience being loved (incoming love), it's because we don't feel lovable, and so we don't recognize it when it comes our way. Usually, when we don't experience being loving (outgoing love), it's because we haven't taken any in in order to give some out —our supply is depleted. And sometimes folks aren't loving because they simply don't know how.

So, let's look at some of the things that love is. And isn't. And can be, though not necessarily.

Love is:
    accepting
    affirming
    permitting
    liberating—no strings, no expectations, no demands
    empowering to lover *and* beloved
    seeing clearly
    feeling solid and real
    feeling exultant
    timeless—no beginning and no end
    abundantly available
    effortless
    self-fulfilling—love begets love begets love begets love,
       etc.
    me knowing you and you knowing me without judging
    being friends
    the feeling I have when I hug a puppy
    purring

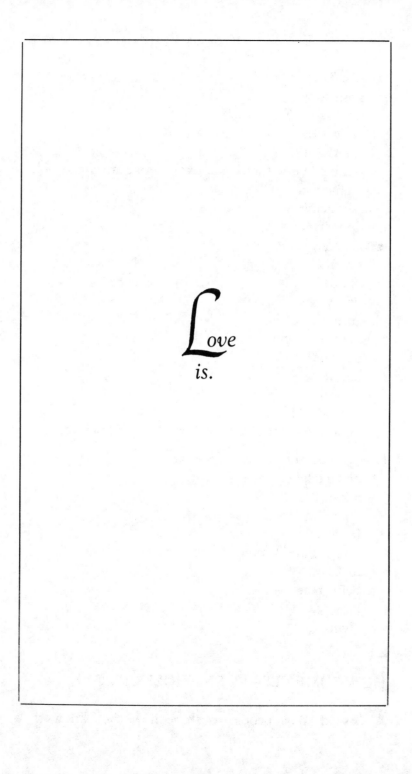

Love
is.

Love isn't:
    possessing
    jealous
    obligating
    smothering
    I can't live without you—you broke my heart—cha, cha, cha
    sacrificing
    doing favors
    Hershey kisses
    romance
    blind
    needy
    greedy
    in short supply
    demanding
    limiting
    critical
    judgmental
    exclusive—limited to 1 or 2 or 12 or 1000 beloveds

Love can be, though isn't necessarily:
    being taken care of
    taking care of
    reliability
    intimacy
    hugging and kissing
    fucking
    being nice
    being good
    giving gifts

HOW SOME PEOPLE EXPERIENCE LOVE

We asked some people to share how they know that

they're experiencing love in their actions, mind, body and perhaps, spirit.

TINA:

When I love, I feel somehow larger than myself. I am forgiving of errors in myself and the person I love—not because of generosity, but because they are too trivial in the light of love's power. Whatever is *not* too trivial, I deal with then—because I care.

My vision gains magnification, too. I see small parts of people (gestures, body parts, thought processes, phrases of speech) in great detail, and they are very beautiful for their uniqueness.

I feel pride—not personal possessive pride, but pride in our humanity—man/woman can be so beautiful.

I feel excitement—sometimes overwhelming, like great waves, sometimes soothing, like ripples lapping at my boat and rocking it.

I feel ferocity. I sometimes want to crush the person I love, because soft gestures do not feel strong enough to express the power of my feelings. (This seems especially true around small babies and animals, who need gentle handling.)

I feel joy—grins, guffaws and giggles. A warm glow seems to fill the space I love in.

I will defend the person I love, from others, from him/herself, from *myself*—which is usually the hardest to see.

With all this power, joy, ferocity and expansion comes peace. The "peace that passes understanding." A sureness about myself, others and my world.

*L*ove
is
free

*(don't settle for expensive
imitations).*

When I love, I am congruent, focused and sure.

I speak and write with an eloquence born of certainty: a clarity which grows out of unself-conscious absorption in the object(s) of my love.

I flow in and out of this state-of-being. I move into possessiveness, anger, lust, distance, pride-of-ownership and many other ways of relating—and I usually know the difference.

RILEY:

Experiencing love is a lifelong growing experience for me. I think that expanding and increasing my ability to experience love is my life's work and that the ultimate experience of pure love is *satori*.

My physical experience of love is a warmth and swelling in my heart. It fills my chest and radiates outward from my body and downward and upward to fill the rest of me. I feel heat and pressure as if my blood pressure goes up (I've never checked my blood pressure at the time). Sometimes this feeling is accompanied by copious tears.

My extra-physical sensation is that I envelop my beloved in the warmth that is radiating from me. This is usually verified by him or her.

My emotional experience of love is a rejoicing when I see, fantasize, or otherwise experience my beloved as separate from me, being her or himself completely and competently. This emotion goes with the swelling warmth in my chest.

I usually experience a sadness with my rejoicing and I think that the sadness is part of saying good-by to the hope that I will own her or him and that I will have a guarantee about someone else taking care of me.

With all this I feel a "rightness" with myself and the world. Everything is in its rightful place.

The moments when I fully experience loving and/or being loved are the high points of my life.

ANNY R:

Love is sneaky sly
creeping into your head and heart
when you least expect it.
Beautiful—
to find someone you didn't know you needed
until one day you realize you'd hate like hell to lose him
even for a moment.

DENTON:

In human loving there are no experts. Love between persons is both dynamic and developmental, and each point of mastery leads to a new beginning—the entry of a new stage. Therefore, the major characteristic of love is growing.

Two people in love experience their feelings with intensity and the intensity spurs their growth. That intensity is recognized in both pleasant and unpleasant sensations. All too often love is retarded by making another's behavior the cause of our sensations. While there is a direct cause-and-effect relationship between others' behavior and our feeling response, each person is responsible for ordering her/his environment so that growth is possible and positive.

Love confronts our current limits and expands our existing capacities to provide and receive and thereby reveals to us new dimensions of our power.

SHERYN:

There are two aspects of love that are recognizable to me. First, in the immediate moment, I am aware of my physical response. I relax and my sensory experience heightens. Colors, sounds and good feelings become vivid. I feel warm, soft, and I experience a rush. Mentally, I'm in touch with the positive in the other person and in me. Emotionally, I feel joyous, excited, moved and movable. I am full of hope and optimism. Generally, love for me is an internal welling up. I become responsive and able to act on my response. There is a flow of energy akin to really being in the here and now and pulsing with that.

The second aspect is over the long run in a relationship. The important feeling here is trust. I feel safe to be myself, knowing I'll be accepted and confronted, if not always liked. I feel free to change and grow and share; to be intimate or far away. I trust that my anger and fears will be dealt with as well as my positive feelings.

TREVOR:

I really know when I'm in love when I don't have to ask myself whether I am or not. A friend once said about love: "If you have to think about it, it isn't there," and I go along with that. Love has a totally unquestioning quality about it. It's when I don't worry about how long it'll last, or why or how, because part of me *knows* that this love is part of the natural order of things, was meant to be, is part of the way the world works. It's when I feel so close to a woman that it feels as if I've known her for years, or maybe even shared a lifetime together centuries ago—that kind of feeling. It's when being together is like "touching base," like going back to one's home town after having been away for a long time.

Being in love means a special, heartfelt quality of sharing, when just being with her or even thinking of her moves me deep down in the same deep, poetic way as when I smell my favorite flowers, or watch a spectacular sunset—that feeling of being connected with the universe, of being totally here enjoying the present moment.

It's love when I meet a woman with whom I feel free to be totally, effortlessly myself. Someone whom I don't have to impress all the time or put on any particular role for, because I just know that she accepts me for me, the way I am.

I used to worship women from afar, putting them on a pedestal. That wasn't love, it was infatuation. These days I know it's real when I meet a woman whom I can have *fun* with too, so that as well as being passionate or gentle or caring or whatever, I also feel free to be my three-year-old, or six-year-old, or 16-year-old, or any age at all . . . able to flow from one to the other. Of course, the other half of that is that the person I'm in love with also feels free to play around like a kid too.

Being in love is when the mere thought of that person makes me feel warm and happy inside, feeling a strong connection even when we're apart, as if when I merely think of her I'm tuning in psychically on her wavelength.

When the thought of being together gives me that same kind of "zing" of energy that goes with a spring day of warm sunshine and showers, when everything is green and growing—that makes me feel *alive*.

Those are the good times. When I *really* know I'm in love is when we hit occasional rough patches and things get difficult and I can *still* feel that the bond of love underneath everything remains solid. So instead of thinking fatalistically, "Well, if we're no longer having fun together, maybe it's time to let this friendship draw to a close," I am willing to dig down deep enough to find out what's going wrong; to explore the misunderstandings, the things that haven't been expressed, or the things that I'm not even aware of because they're buried way down in my unconscious. So for me, being in love means that when difficulties occur in the relationship, instead of retreating and backing away, I care enough to turn around and confront the problem. I become willing to look at my own behavior, willing to re-evaluate set patterns of thinking, willing to consider whether there is any other way to show that I care or to keep the relationship going.

Being in love means wanting wholeheartedly to *be* there for her, to cheer her, to comfort her, to soothe her. Or being willing to give her space if that's what she needs. Being willing to allow her to do what she wants and be what she wants instead of expecting her to do or be what *I* want.

Being in love means wanting to share my life with this person, especially all the nicest, most beautiful things in my life. And the downs, too. When something exciting happens, I want to tell her about it before anyone else. It's wanting to be together and grow together, knowing that each of us is going to keep on growing and changing, and not always in the same direction.

ANNIE U.:

My experience of love comes when I least expect it. Out of empty spaces, quiet times and very ordinary moments emerges an awareness that something new is happening, something warm is in the room, and suddenly I am not alone.

I've known these moments when surrounded by sea and sky and beach on a solitary day. I've known them in sharing with huge crowds and small groups. But mostly I've known them in little glimpses with another person, as we struggle and grow and create together.

In the midst of that struggling and growing and creating, something new happens in the world. Two do not become *one*—it's more like three or four or more! Each two people loving give rise to something new: a unique relationship, a particular entity that has never existed before. With each loving relationship in my life, another completely new thing is created.

Loving is, as Tina and Riley have said, sometimes work. But it is joy, too, and the assurance of that special creation comes just often enough to keep me in the game. At the same time there is enough distance between the assurances to allow things to be open and flowing, rather than stifling and oppressive.

As one contemporary wedding service says, love is what allows us "to keep alive and grow, to maintain our capacity for wonder, spontaneity and humor. It is seeing the meaning of life through the changing prism of our own relationship, and seeing the relationship in the context of the world and all of its limitations and possibilities."

That leads me to a final note. I believe that it is not possible for love to be limited—that's one of *my* biases. For me

*L*ove
thyself
as thou
wouldst
love
thy
neighbor.

that means that love extends itself to caring, at some level, for the hungry, the sick, the prisoners, the alienated ones —the people the world neglects, ignores or oppresses.

LEARNING TO EXPERIENCE LOVE

If experiencing love is a problem for you, here are some suggestions.

First, understand that loving begins with self-love—Love thyself as thou wouldst love thy neighbor. That's right, loving ourselves is the most important thing we can do.

We can't take in love from others unless we believe we are lovable.
And we can't give out love unless we take it in.
Love is a flowing—in and out.
We are a conduit which carries love—in one end (so to speak) and out the other.

So you say, how do I begin the process—how do I learn to love myself?
Start with a puppy. Or an infant.
It's easy to feel pure, uncritical, generous love toward a puppy or a tiny baby.
Do it, in fantasies and in reality.
Practice.

Then, pick a quiet time and place (perhaps before you go to sleep at night or before arising in the morning) and picture the infant (or warm puppy) inside of *you*. This is the you that is lovable. Allow yourself to feel those loving feelings toward that part of you.

Know that that part of you is real and deserves your love, and therefore, anybody's love.

Do it every day for a while.

Now you're ready to take in love, so, begin to take note of any loving word or action which comes your way—at least once a day. Count only the ones that feel good—there is some counterfeit love out there, and it's hard for a beginner to tell the difference.

Now that you're noticing what loving words and actions are, you will probably begin to give them out spontaneously. It is impossible to hoard love.

There are many folks who don't seem to be able to get the hang of it. They are just certain that they're not lovable. (And somewhat scared about it too.) If you're one of those people, a good therapist or counselor—one who knows about loving—can probably help you find your lovableness. Even if you can't find it, it's there—and an expert can show you where.

CHAPTER 12

THE OPEN SEXUAL COUPLE

Those of us who are looking for freedom in our couple relationships often consider whether or not to include freedom to have sexual intimacy with friends other than our partners.

We (Riley and Tina) believe that any experience is potentially a learning experience, no matter how painful, and that the pain is the result of our resistance to encountering our blind spots or unexamined beliefs. We believe that stretching the boundaries of our loving relationships and stretching the boundaries of our beliefs about ourselves and the world are the ways people learn and grow.

We do not believe that people SHOULD experiment with open sexual agreements. We do believe that it is appropriate at some times and with some couples, and that only you know (or suspect) when that time is for you—if ever. We offer the following as a guide for the experiment, if you choose to experience open sexuality.

Sexual intimacy outside our partnership, like any expression of personal freedom, challenges and flexes our feelings of self-worth and our ability to love.

If our partner has sex with someone else, we can choose to feel:

rejected, abandoned or unloved.

worried about what people think.

inadequate because we don't meet ALL our partner's needs.

deprived of our "exclusive rights."

betrayed.

threatened.

ugly.

insecure.

like a failure.

abandoned and hopeless.

There's a lot of social pressure "out there" and in our heads to think and feel these ways.

We also have the option to temper these thoughts and feelings with our unqualified love and an understanding of our basic worth and lovableness and a sense of adventure.

Then, we could choose to feel:

enriched by the experience (not losing our partner, but gaining a new dear friend).

generous and giving.

courageous and experimental.

free to make our own new contacts.

in charge of our own destiny.

unconditionally loving.

spiritually guided.

growing and learning.

and a hundred other positive attitudes.

SO, WHAT'S TO DO?

1. Do it as a "partnership" or it won't work. A mutual sense of adventure and love is important. It will help you stay on track, give purpose to your activities and make the

painful times bearable. Remember that you are blazing new trails and pushing the limits of love and emotional maturity. Hold a vision of unconditional love.

If one partner wants to open up the relationship and the other partner doesn't, that's an issue for Cooperative Problem Solving. The process of clarifying wants and looking at options are powerful exercises in this situation (see pages 89–98). Don't let fear of apparent scarcity frighten you into abrupt moves or power plays that can damage the trust and cooperation you need to do this together. If you do something rash, be willing to back up and do it over, with caring feelings for your partner.

2. Be prepared to confront your worst fears. You will probably be surprised at what ideas and feelings emerge. The idea here is to remember that feeling afraid and acting out of fear does not mean that you are doing something wrong. Expect it and flow with it. Don't fight it or pretend you don't feel it. It is easy to get stuck when this happens, and sometimes it is necessary to get help and support from a professional therapist. Be aware that many therapists, in keeping with the "traditional rules" in our culture, don't believe it's possible. Find one who is accepting of open sexual relationships, knows they can work, and is not prejudiced against what you are doing. The sex information hotline in your nearest city can usually help you find someone.

3. Find a support community. Access to people who are living your desired lifestyle is invaluable. Not only will you broaden your circle of friends, you will also have a source of validation and encouragement and role models, as well as advice when the going gets rough.

4. Be prepared to focus on your relationship a lot, especially at first. Spend extra time nurturing your love together and reassuring each other. Spend extra time

problem solving. The attitudes and skills delineated in this book become *very* important.

5. Remember to work with a very specific, real situation that exists right now. Do not negotiate agreements for hypothetical cases in the future. In our experience, hypothetical cases are terrifying. We conjure up all kinds of idealized and therefore threatening people for our partner to be with. Whereas if my partner is talking about Jan at work, I can see that Jan's an ordinary person, and my partner can reassure me in very specific ways. "I don't want Jan for a partner, even though I like Jan a lot and I'm turned on. I want you for a partner and I have no intention of changing my mind about that."

But what if my partner isn't sure about staying with me? What if Jan turns out to be more attractive than I am?

We can only negotiate one problem at a time. So, let's look at the first question: "What if my partner isn't sure about staying with me?" The problem here seems to be indecision, and the solution lies in clarifying wants.

At this point, it is necessary to follow a specific want in order to get to a solution. Let's say that my partner wants to be sexually excited more often and wants to be complimented and feel sexually exciting. One could get this with an occasional new lover, by "flirting" without following through, or by working out some new options within the relationship. There are probably other choices, too. The point is, the problem is now clearly solvable, and it only remains for the two partners (and perhaps Jan) to decide which solution they prefer.

Now the second question, "What if Jan turns out to be more attractive than I am?" is an example of a hypothetical situation in the future. It's the kind of question we scare ourselves with. And it can't be negotiated until it comes up. The essence of the scare is, "If we have an open relationship, you may find someone you like better than me." We don't know a way around that one. It can't be negotiated, because it isn't specific and it's in the future. We believe that if an open sexual relationship (or any free-couple relationship) is to succeed, it must be done one day, one problem (and one success) at a time. There are always unknowns in life and usually some way to handle them when they arise.

When the problem is REAL and NOW, it can be solved. We believe that there is enough to go around. Everyone CAN get what they want.

CHAPTER 13

SEXUAL FREEDOM AND HEALTH

With the advent of herpes and AIDS, there has been a change in the Sexual Revolution, and a backlash. Of course we are concerned. Experimenting with sexual freedom and intimacy has now become a gamble with high stakes.

We have all been frightened about AIDS and other diseases, may of us to the point of despair. There is a lot of misleading and frightening information bombarding us. This chapter is intended to give you the best facts we have about AIDS and how to remain safe. The same practices that minimize the AIDS risk also protect against contracting herpes and other diseases. Our information is from Project AHEAD, a Los Angeles based organization in the forefront of AIDS education, and is up to date at this writing.

AIDS (Acquired Immune Deficiency Syndrome) is a physical condition brought about by a virus, currently called HIV (Human Immune Virus). The virus attacks the T-cells in the blood, the cells which, in effect, direct the body's immune response. Once the immune response is weakened, many infections, such as pneumonia and certain types of cancer, can easily attack and overwhelm the body. The patient does not actually die of AIDS, but of the cumulative effects of all these infections. Although there have been several reported cases of recovery from AIDS, the disease is currently considered fatal.

SEXUAL FREEDOM AND HEALTH

Because AIDS has been found largely in certain groups in this country (the demographics are different in other countries, such as Africa) we have heard a lot about "high-risk" groups. However, it is very important to know that it is not actually the characteristics of the group (such as being gay, promiscuous, or an IV drug user) that puts them at risk. The risk comes from their behavior. ANYONE CAN PLACE THEMSELF AT RISK BY THEIR ACTIVITIES, AND ANYONE CAN REMOVE THEMSELF FROM RISK BY CHANGING THEIR ACTIVITIES.

Physical, mental and emotional stress all reduce the efficiency of your immune system. So, to remain safe, it is important to reduce chronic stress, and many of the safety guidelines that follow are intended to help you do so. In addition, be aware that the HIV virus is passed through blood-to-blood or semen-to-blood contact. There is no evidence that AIDS can be contracted from normal social contact, friendly kissing, hugging, shaking hands, hot tubs or toilet seats.

Here are Project AHEAD'S guidelines for removing yourself from risk:

Know your sex partners (this will reduce your stress as well as your chances of exposure).

Negotiate an agreement about how you will keep yourselves safe. You can't afford to be shy.

Reduce the number of partners (this will also reduce stress and chances of exposure).

Use condoms (latex condoms, with Nonoxynol 9 spermicide, are considered most effective. Educate yourself about proper use from your doctor or a counselor such as Planned Parenthood).

Don't use unsterile or shared needles, razor blades or toothbrushes.

Avoid oral contact with fecal matter, semen and urine (because you may not be aware of bleeding gums, or blood in the body secretions).

Stop or reduce the use of drugs, tobacco and alcohol (these are immune suppressants—use moderately). Antibiotics are also powerful immune suppressants—use only when absolutely necessary, under a doctor's supervision.

Most important, KEEP YOUR IMMUNE SYSTEM STRONG AND HEALTHY:

> exercise regularly
> eat a good diet
> get plenty of rest
> reduce emotional stress.

None of these precautions are difficult or require you to live joylessly. In fact, fun is a great disease preventer—it releases accumulated stress. If you know you aren't taking good care of your health and you can't seem to change your habits, that's an issue for counseling. Get yourself help with that, before you need help with your health!

If you believe your past activities have placed you at risk, you may want to go through HIV antibody testing. If you do, please get tested only at a center that provides counseling about AIDS along with the test. Testing without supportive counseling is counterproductive. No matter what your results are, you'll get good, positive counseling about AIDS prevention and how to take care of yourself. There are many supportive, reassuring programs in our cities which have good information. Call your local Department of Health for a referral. You deserve to know how to keep yourself healthy.

The only thing you need to change is your risky behavior. Mutual masturbation, for example, is a good way to replace riskier sex practices when you are having sex with many partners you do not know well. If you are in ANYTHING other than a monogamous relationship, or are not sure, please follow the guidelines above.

We have heard much talk that the "sexual revolution" is over. Actually, we believe there is a new and better revolution in the making, and we call it the Safer Sexual Revolution. We still believe in freedom, and we still believe in the importance of the health of the individual. We hope the preceding information helps you make your choices safely.

CHAPTER 14

THE FREE COUPLE

Throughout this book, we (Tina and Riley) have insisted that people set their own standards for their couple relationships—that each of us must define our own freedom and our own goals. We feel that freedom is inherently individual—that because no two humans are identical, no two humans can be free in exactly the same way.

At the same time, our bias is present. We *do* have a picture of an ideal free couple in our heads. Our individual ideals differ slightly, yet they are similar enough so that we have helped each other define our wants and needs. Consequently, we each have a clear understanding of the other's ideal. And in fact, the ideas and techniques we've described up to now came out of our search to implement our own ideals.

In order to bring our ideals into the open, and perhaps to influence your thinking, here is a synthesis of Riley and Tina's ideas of what constitutes a "free couple."

First, they love each other. Love flows freely between them and is readily accessible. They both know they love and they both know they *are* loved.

Second, they have agreed on their goal(s) for coupling. They have a sense of purpose, and coupling is one way to achieve that purpose. Perhaps their goal is to furnish a "home base" for one another—a place where they can rest and rejuvenate themselves after stressful work in the "rat race." Perhaps it's to raise kids in a particular way. Perhaps their coupling is in order to challenge themselves to change and grow—a person who tends to nest and wants to learn to venture forth could couple with someone who tends to venture and wants to learn about nesting. Their relationship may involve a lot of conflict and struggle leading to growth.

We do not assume that "easy is best." Again, individual goals reflect individual situations. People grow where they feel motivated. If I am in a challenging, draining career, I may want an "easy," unchallenging, supportive relationship. In that case, I am learning a lot of career-oriented skills and few relationship skills. I already have the skills I need to relate to my partner. Perhaps, at a later date, I will switch emphasis and want more challenge at home—all solutions (agreements) are negotiable at any time.

Third, our ideal couple have a clear commitment to each other and to themselves: "I will love you no matter what and support you in whatever your heart desires, and we will be together and learn together and with others until our purpose is achieved. I will share my bad (unsatisfied, unsuccessful, unhappy) feelings with you, so that you can offer me help and understanding. In that way, we will both feel we can get what we want, and will be working together toward success."

Fourth, our ideal couple are realistic. They do not expect themselves or each other to be perfect. They do not look upon feeling bad as someone's error, but as a signal that their relationship (or one of them) needs attention. They do *not* compete with each other to see who can "win." They *do* cooperate and rejoice in each other's gains and successes. They do *not* nit-pick, seeing each small incident as crucial to their success. They *do* examine their attitudes when problems arise, intent on solving the problem to their mutual advantage.

Fifth, they recognize challenge and struggle as indicators of personal (and mutual) growth. They realize that their freedom can look strange to other couples and they support each other when challenged by the "normal" couples. They learn to explain their unusual relationship (when desirable) without feeling superior to more conventional couples.

They feel:
> free
> loving
> loved
> courageous
> intelligent
> challenged
> aware
> focused
> successful
> committed
> energized
> secure
> powerful
> good
>> most of the time.

That is our ideal. What about some other types of free couples? As we said, we're biased. Yet we can still imagine relationships different from our ideal which could be ideal for others. Also, we have examples from other writers.

Dick Sutphen writes in *You Were Born Again to Be Together*: "Being totally idealistic, what would real love be like? To begin with, it could not be diminished by anything the other person said or did. Your love would not be dependent upon being loved. You would give freely, without any expectation of return. In an environment of real love, you would allow total freedom to your mate, expecting no more than the other could give. You would love for what the other was. You would not expect your mate to change, to be something he or she was not. You would find joy in the other's happiness. To really love someone, you need to be complete within yourself, without fear. You then will find joy in the positive aspects of your relationship and allow the negatives to simply flow past you without affecting you.

Most of us are far from attaining true love. Even if we believe in it, it is sometimes hard to live it. But what a beautiful relationship this involved detachment would be."[1]

Claude Steiner in *Scripts People Live*: "Example: A man and a woman meet at the park. Their innermost wishes are quite similar to each other's. They both want to hold hands, run in the grass, stroke each other's hair, touch each other's skin and talk about themselves to each other. Were they acting freely, they would proceed to do so and continue until one or the other decided to stop, and then their relationship would change or end."[2]

Kahlil Gibran, in *The Prophet*: "Love one another, but make not a bond of love:
Let it rather be a moving sea between the shores of your souls.
Fill each other's cup but drink not from one cup.

[1](New York: Pocket Books, 1976), p. 252.
[2](New York: Grove Press, 1974), p. 316.

*The strings of
a lute
are alone though
they quiver
with the same
music.*

—Gibran

Give one another of your bread but eat not from the same
  loaf.
Sing and dance together and be joyous, but let each one of
    you be alone/Even as the strings of a lute are alone
    though they quiver with the same music.
Give your hearts, but not into each other's keeping.
For only the hand of love can contain your hearts.
And stand together yet not too near together.
For the pillars of the temple stand apart,
And the oak tree and the cypress grow not in each other's
    shadow."[3]

Does all this mean that we think conventional coupling is
wrong? Not necessarily. We can conceive of and have wit-
nessed "conventional" couples who are happy and who
feel free and successful. Either the social rules for coupling
match their own wants, or they have managed to alter
them subtly to allow themselves the freedom they need
without making themselves conspicuous.

There are many possibilities for the free couple. The very
definition of "free couple" encourages many options.

THAT IS THE POINT.

OPTIONS.

The free couple has many choices. They are not bound to
Mom and Dad's version of marriage. Or anybody else's.
So, we postulate the "career couples":

He goes to medical school, she works to put him through.
Later, she goes to school if she wants to. They both feel
fairly treated.

She has a career on the stage. He is her manager, producer
and agent. She gets the publicity, he is really the force
behind her. They both feel successful.

[3](New York: Alfred A. Knopf, n.d.), p. 15.

They both have professional careers and have professional help with housework, etc. They use their relationship and their home as a recharging place, discussing their problems and successes equally. They feel important to each other.

She is a politician. He helps her campaign and makes speeches to support her programs when she's in office. He advises her and keeps his "ear to the ground." They feel dedicated to the same goals.

He is a business man. She's a housewife and mother. She helps his career with dinner parties, etc. They feel successful and congruent.

The less career-oriented:

He has a part-time job servicing appliances. She works as a secretary and earns two thirds of the money. He has more time, so he takes care of most of the housework and child rearing. They feel appropriate to each other.

They're gypsies, traveling around various countries, doing travelogues to earn money. They feel adventurous and cooperative.

They both have routine jobs and are involved in a hobby, such as folk dancing. They organize much of their time around dance-club activities. They enjoy each other.

They are wealthy. She devotes time to charities, he raises horses. They share each other's private worlds. They feel intellectually stimulated.

They are farmers, or pioneers. They share the work and have all they can handle. They feel fruitful and indispensible to each other.

They are very religious. They devote their lives to spreading the gospel. She preaches, he directs the music and organizes their meetings. They feel mutually inspired.

*L*et us support
      one another
let us learn from
      one another
let us love
      one another
without expectations.

We could go on and on. We could change the "he's and she's" in each of the prior examples. The possibilities abound. This is the springboard. You are now free to use it in your own way.

Play with the "couple types." If you are presently in a couple relationship, or have had one in the past, write it up as though it were to be included in this chapter. Then look at it. How does it suit you?

Look at our examples and the quotes on coupling. What do you like? What sounds awful? Remember, you are a free person. All you need to do is act on your freedom. Use all your imagination, all your communication, all your cooperation and all your love.

We wish you success and freedom—whatever they mean to *you*.

ABOUT THE AUTHORS

Riley K. Smith and Tina B. Tessina, licensed Marriage and Family Counselors, are psychotherapists in private practice in Southern California. They are close friends and have worked together and separately, teaching, leading therapy groups and training therapist-interns since 1975. *How to Be a Couple and Still Be Free* was a successful course for two years before it became a book.

Out of their therapy practice, couples classes and workshops, their group living experience, their own no-holds-barred friendship, and their own separate couple relationships, the authors have developed the view about relationships which led to the insights and techniques described in this book. Tina has also written *Lovestyles: How to Celebrate Your Differences* (Newcastle, 1987).

For information about counseling or workshops, call Tina in Long Beach at (213) 438-8077 or Riley in Los Angeles at (213) 390-1737.